OCCASIONAL CONTRIBUTIONS FROM THE MUSEUM OF
ANTHROPOLOGY OF THE UNIVERSITY OF MICHIGAN
NO. 13

GREEN CORN CEREMONIALISM
IN
THE EASTERN WOODLANDS

BY
JOHN WITTHOFT

ANN ARBOR
UNIVERSITY OF MICHIGAN PRESS
1949

© 1949 by the Regents of the University of Michigan
The Museum of Anthropology
All rights reserved

ISBN (print): 978-1-949098-51-8
ISBN (ebook): 978-1-951538-50-7

Browse all of our books at
sites.lsa.umich.edu/archaeology-books.

Order our books from the University of Michigan
Press at www.press.umich.edu.

For permissions, questions, or manuscript queries,
contact Museum publications by email at umma-pubs@umich.edu or visit the Museum website at
lsa.umich.edu/ummaa.

CONTENTS

Introduction 1
The Algonkian Peoples of New England and New York . . 6
The Delaware and Southeastern Algonkians 11
The Iroquois 21
The Cherokee 31
The Southeastern Siouan Tribes 50
The Creek Indians and Their Neighbors 52
The Natchez and Tribes Outside of the Eastern Woodlands Area 70
Corn Origin Myths 77
Conclusion 82
Literature Cited 85

INTRODUCTION[1]

For some centuries prior to the appearance of Europeans on the North American continent, the aboriginal peoples of the Eastern Woodlands and of the eastern plains shared an economic cultural complex that depended largely upon agriculture and chiefly upon one plant, *Zea mays* L., for its staple. The colonists quickly adopted this agricultural complex, and today we still use techniques of agriculture that are native American in origin (the hilling of corn, for example, and the planting of pumpkins, squash, and beans in corn hills), whereas in Europe, American plants were broadcast or planted in rows, the traditional methods of European grain culture. It is interesting to note that some of the American Indians first planted rice in hills, rather than in rows or broadcast in fields.[2] Along with traditional and complex techniques for the cultivation of these crops, however, the aborigines also possessed a large body of folk-belief and ritual which was an integral part of their maize complex. It was precisely this phase of Indian agriculture which the white colonists did not adopt; in fact, they seem to have been only slightly aware of its existence and never seem to have noticed it as an American equivalent of the European complex of agricultural beliefs, festivals, and magical practices with which they were familiar. One still notes, in the folklore of white American communities, survivals of European practices of planting by the moon, of European festivals having agricultural significance, in addition to many similar vestiges of an extinct folk agricultural complex, grafted on the part of their agricultural economy that is largely of American origin.

At the time of the colonization of America, many parts of Europe still preserved an integrated cycle of festivals, popular observances, and supernaturalistic practices directly concerned

[1] This study is revised from a master's thesis in anthropology presented to the University of Pennsylvania in June, 1946. I wish to thank Dr. Frank G. Speck, Dr. William N. Fenton, Mr. Merle Deardorff, and Mr. Volney Jones for their helpful suggestions and criticism.

[2] Bartram, 1853, p. 48; Hawkins, 1848, p. 66.

with the agricultural year, a complex which had survived until very recent times, but which now exists almost entirely as a cherished memory of the folklorist. This religio-magical complex is certainly as worthy of study by the ethnologist as any comparable systems from other parts of the world and presents a basic pattern not too unlike corresponding agricultural complexes of other cultures. James Frazer, in *The Golden Bough*, attempted a reconstruction from the European and Mediterranean material of this sort, which he has used to interpret similar complexes in Asia, Africa, and the Americas and in turn reinterpreted European data in terms of conclusions drawn from the other continents. Earlier observers of the American Indian had fallen into the same pattern of fanciful treatment and had frequently looked to Hebrew, Tartar, or Middle American parallels for the origin of the Indian festivals they observed. In no case did an observer conclude that he had seen one item of a comparable and nonrelated system which would present a very different picture if he had collected more data. Later ethnological investigators did not commit such gross errors of judgment, but they rarely attempted to gather enough information to justify more objective conclusions.

Actually, today there is not enough data on the nonmaterial aspects of the agriculture of most of the eastern tribes to attempt a synthetic picture of the maize complex of any particular people. We do have indications that information which is now available existed as part of an integrated system of belief and practice, a pattern perhaps comparable in complexity, elaboration, and interest to the well-described European system which has been mentioned. It seems hopeless, however, to attempt to fit these fragments together into an understandable whole. The processes of acculturation are bringing the same destruction to Indian cultures that they have brought to older European folk-belief, yet even modern ethnographies dealing with the eastern areas do not emphasize the survivals and modified units of these agricultural complexes that still remain. Students of this area have also failed to elucidate the maize complex, in both its material and nonmaterial aspects, as a set of related phenomena possessing some unity in each culture.

A very interesting and difficult historical problem is suggested by these ideas. It is known from the archaeology of the eastern United States that maize agriculture is of no great antiquity in this area. Most authorities date the introduction of maize into the Eastern Woodlands as not earlier than 500 A.D.[3] The area of maize cultivation in eastern North America is geographically separated from the nearest occurrence, in the Southwest, by a nonagricultural area. Within this eastern area are uniformly distributed specific material traits concerned with maize cultivation which are not characteristic of areas farther south and west in the Americas. These include the hoe, replaced in other areas by the digging stick and the foot plow[4] (spade); the corn mortar and pestle (present in some Mexican areas); the use of mats of braided corn husks (the ears are braided together to hang for drying and storage; later the corn is removed for use, and the braids are utilized); the use of corn as hominy (shell leached from the kernels with potash from wood ashes); corn bread wrapped in corn leaves and baked in ashes; and use of a wooden dish of special shape for mixing corn-bread dough, a utensil which may possibly be descended from a pre-agricultural type of soapstone bowl of the same shape found archaeologically throughout most of this area. Irrigation was not practical in this area. Botanical study of the maize varieties of the eastern United States also supports this conclusion, as noted especially in the studies of Carter,[5] who finds a concentric distribution of corn varieties in this area, with the oldest varieties in the North, correlated with the stratigraphic position of similar varieties in the Southwest. Carter's conclusions about the ultimate origins of maize cultivation are not of concern here, except that they support the theory of the uniform diffusion of maize agriculture throughout eastern North America from a single direction.

It seems probable that the diffusion of maize within this eastern province would not have represented merely the borrowing of seed corn by the neighbors of agricultural peoples and

[3] Webb and Snow, 1945, p. 312; Ritchie, 1944, p. 323.
[4] Linton, 1924; Wissler, 1922, pp. 19-23.
[5] Carter, 1945, pp. 39-55.

their handing on seed to their neighbors. In actuality a real maize complex would have been diffused, including specific techniques for the growing and utilization of maize, knowledge of its botanical peculiarities (such as its inability to reproduce itself by self-sowing, and its tendency to grow extra "prop-roots" when dirt is hilled around the base of the plant), a set of magical and ritual precepts and traditions directly concerned with the cultivation and utilization of maize, and mythological and folktale material concerning the origin, nature, history, and use of maize. Such a nonmaterial culture complex would no doubt be distorted and modified in the transmission. It might be adjusted to, and combined with, existing institutions and come to present a somewhat differing entity in each cultural setting. It might later be modified or even replaced by the diffusion of other systems of belief or come to fulfill a differing function in each cultural group and so start a specific evolution of its own. The impetus given to an already existing culture by a new and more productive economy might also result in the evolution of a new ceremonial pattern from preagricultural systems of ritual. Later developments and modifications within small ethnic groups might come to influence the culture of large sections of the area.

Since the technology centered about maize shows a rather similar basic pattern throughout the eastern United States and a somewhat different pattern from that of other areas, a comparative study of nonmaterial aspects of maize agriculture might be justifiable. Unfortunately, as I have previously indicated, material for such a study is rather sparse in comparison to the information on many other phases of the cultures of this area. Perhaps future ethnographic study may contribute enough data to make such a survey more feasible, but the amount of survival of aboriginal traits of this sort may be very small. For this reason I intend to restrict this study to one particular ritual, the one about which most is known and which seems to have been of major significance.

There are enough data from most parts of the eastern United States to indicate that three major festivals were immediately concerned with the cultivation of corn, but in few areas is there further information. Two of these ceremonies, the planting ceremony and the harvest festival, seem to have been of secondary importance and did not attract much attention among observers. The so-called green corn dance, however, seems to have been the most significant to the aborigines, and much fuller accounts of it from several areas exist. Recent ethnographic studies of this ceremony from several tribes have also been made, and there is a sense of its homogeneity throughout fairly large geographic areas. It was a ceremony held when the green corn was first edible, and, at least in some areas, marked a major division of the year. The time of its occurrence would make historical connection between the same rite in different areas more likely, for the coincidence of such rites as planting and harvest festivals as parallel developments in different cultures would be more expected. It is surprising that neither of these rituals was selected for the place of first importance and for elaboration by the aboriginal maize farmers.

The problem in this particular ceremony is severalfold. First, I intend to indicate the distribution of this rite, and then, by comparative study, to point out similarities and differences between different areas, and point to some evidence of historical connection. The second problem is to note special modifications and differences in function of this ritual as found in the different ethnic groups. These two lines of inquiry, however, would be difficult to separate and will be pursued together. Finally, as a sort of philosophic background for the ceremony, I should like to introduce a distributional study of the Corn Mother myths and point to some possible relationships between these tales and the ceremony with which I am chiefly concerned.

The ideal method for the study of green corn ceremonialism would no doubt be to chart and plot the distribution of all traits associated with the green corn ceremonies and then to analyze these trait distributions. In view of the limited amount of data for most areas, however, such a study could include only a small part of the traits actually characteristic of each locality's ritual. The data are generally too sparse to permit the necessary evaluation of such traits as might be considered diagnostic. This study does not presume to offer a final trait-distribution study. The object has been to interpret the data available as carefully as possible in terms of two hypotheses: first, the green corn ceremonies of the various peoples in the Eastern Woodlands are historically connected phenomena; second, these rituals have been subjected to considerable elaboration and specialization in different locales. Some attention is also given to the possible place of origin of green corn rituals.

THE ALGONKIAN PEOPLES OF NEW ENGLAND AND NEW YORK

THE data for the area of Algonkian peoples are sparse. For New England, especially, there is very little information on agricultural ceremonies. In northern New England maize cultivation seems to have been an irregular and speculative venture, but according to John Gyles's *Captivity* the Malecite were growing maize in the St. Johns Valley about 1686; he described some of the ceremonial life of the people among whom he was a captive, but mentioned nothing comparable to the corn ceremonialism.[6] It seems probable that such festival observances as the green corn ceremony were lacking in the cultures of this area, on the margin of practical maize cultivation. Chamberlain mentioned a Malecite (?) tradition of a green corn dance from the Penobscot of Indian Island, Maine, but it seems probable that the tradition was handed down from a non-Malecite (Iroquois?) source.[7] This is the same area from which the mortar and pestle and other ethnological traits of the maize complex are missing.[8]

The earliest reference to what would appear to be a green corn festival in New England is the Narraganset account of Roger Williams:

> But their chiefest Idoll of all for sport and game, is (if their land be at peace) toward Harvest when they set up a long house called Qurnekamuck which signifies *Longhouse*, sometimes a hundred, sometimes two hundred feet long upon a plaine near the Court (which they

[6] Gyles, 1851, p. 83.　[7] Chamberlain, 1904, p. 285.
[8] Speck, 1940, pp. 93-94.

call Kittsickanick) where many thousands, men and women meet, where he that goes in danceth in the sight of all the rest; and is prepared with money, coasts, small breeches, knives, or what he is able to reach to, and gives these things away to the poor, who yet must particularly beg and say, Cowegustummous, that is, I beseech you: which word (although there is not one common beggar amongst them) yet they all often use when their richest amongst them would obtain ought by gift.[9]

The other reference to this Narraganset festival reveals little except the date for its observance. In July, 1689 (these dates are old-style), an Indian war was feared in this part of New England, and it was believed that Ninegrat, a Narraganset chief, was laying plans for warfare at a series of Indian festivals. In a Hartford, Connecticut, manuscript is a reference to one of these ceremonies:

Relation of Goodwife Osborn that the war had been planned at the dance at Robin's Town and would be concluded at the great dance at Ninecrafts, which would be held when 'greene Indian corn was high anufe to make their bread of.'[10]

The chief was questioned, and the following bit of testimony seems to relate to this festival, indicating the use of a bark-covered structure:

Hee says hee sent for two Indians named Cajanottore, a Narragansett Indian, that now lives at Pocasset, and Nattawhahore, formerly a Cononicut Indian, now at Pocasset, because hee knew they were formerly his Indians, and had skill to bark cedar trees and to make bark houses, which he men had not good skill in, and that they had gott the barks, but being disturbed by these troubles had not used them.[11]

In the succeeding testimony are references to the major ceremony at which the English feared the materialization of

[9] Williams, 1827, pp. 146–47.
[10] MS "Indian Papers," I: 17; quotation kindly supplied by Mrs. Eva Butler.
[11] *Rhode Island Historical Society Collection*, 2 (1829): 272.

this plot:

> Hee, being demanded what was the reason for this great dance, replied; it is known to you it is noe unusual thing for us soe to doe; but that it is often used from the time after the weeding of our corne till such time as wee doe eat of it; and farther said it was a kind of invocation used among them, that they might have a plentiful harvest.[12]
>
> And as to his present making a great dance, hee answered it was knowne to us, that it was noe unusual practice; it being their manner of Invocation in the time of the growing of their corne, until it was neere riped, that they might receive a plentiful harvest....[13]

It seems probable that similar green corn festivals were known among most tribes of southern New England, but references are scant. We have one older mention of a green corn festival among the Mohegan of eastern Connecticut, and a recent description of a broken-down survival of this ritual. Ezra Stiles recorded one mention of the Mohegan green corn festival:

> Aged Mr. Waterman, born 1708, in 1790 tells me that aet. ten he was present at an Indian Powwaw at Mohegan—and also at New Corn Feast at which last they danced all night—no Sacrifice of Animals.[14]

The Mohegan still preserved some remnant of this ceremony in the first decade of the twentieth century. Frank G. Speck participated in a number of these meetings and has recorded a brief description of the procedure:

> There is no doubt, however, that the Mohegan, like most of the Atlantic coast sedentary tribes, had a ceremony to signalize the season of the corn harvest. This ceremony, known widely among other tribes as the Green Corn Dance, has a degraded survival in a modern September festival. The festival is now simply a sort of fair for the benefit of the Indian Church. A suitable time is appointed, and the men proceed to erect a large wigwam as a shelter. An area adjoining the church at least sixty feet square, is covered by this arbor. Crotched chestnut posts are erected in the ground about ten feet apart, and,

---

[12] *Ibid.*, p. 273.   [13] *Ibid.*, p. 277.   [14] Stiles, 1916, p. 409.

from one to the other of these, crosspieces are laid, a construction previously described (p. 188). Quantities of green white birch saplings have been cut and are then strewn over the roof quite thickly. The sides are filled and woven in with these also, in such a manner as to make a fairly weather tight enclosure. A portion of the wigwam's side is visible in the background of plate XXXI. For some days before the festival, several men are kept busy pounding up quantities of corn for yokeg which the women and children have roasted. Several large mortars are kept exclusively for this purpose, and are the common property of the tribe. The days of the festival are merely the occasion for a general informal gathering of the Indians from far and near, and the sale, for the benefit of the church treasury, of such things as they are able to make. Many articles of Indian manufacture already described are displayed on benches in this wigwam, for sale as souvenirs and articles of utility; while various dishes of food, ancient and modern are made and sold on the grounds. Some other kind of amusement is usually introduced from outside for the three days and an admission price is charged. They also have someone appear in full Indian costume as an added attraction. The Mohegan make this annual gathering a sort of national holiday. The fact it takes place at the height of the corn season, and that corn products, particularly yokeg and suktac, play such an important part in it, are clear indications of the early nature of this festival.[15]

Speck has elsewhere published a photograph of the "wigwam" built in 1909 for this occasion[16] and has personally supplied additional data concerning the structure. It was rectangular, flat-roofed, at least sixty feet long, and built against the church, so that the front wall and one side wall of the church formed parts of two sides of the "wigwam," the whole church being enclosed in the rectangle. The back door of the church opened into this structure, and the other door, on the opposite side of the bower, was overlapped like the entrance to a New England Indian stockade. This building, really a bower longhouse, may be typical of certain ceremonial structures in southern New England, and may have been associated with the green corn festival in some localities.

The proper name for the festival was "wigwam." The women

[15] Speck, 1909a, pp. 194–95.   [16] Speck, 1928, p. 258 (Plate 36).

decided when the corn was ripe enough for the "wigwam" to be held. Proceeds from the festival and from the articles sold went to the church, suggesting a transference of the gift association noted by Roger Williams.

One early New York reference, recorded by Daniel Denton in 1670, is from Long Island, an area most closely related ethnically to southern New England. His description is probably from his own observations, but the details are quite vague, and the account shows small understanding:

> For their worship which is diabolical, it is performed usually but once or twice a year, unless upon some extraordinary occasion, as upon making war or the like; their usual time is about *Michaelmass*, when their corn is first ripe, the day being appointed by their chief Priest or pawwaw; most of them go a hunting for venison: when they are all congregated, their priest tells them if he wants money, their God will accept of no other offering, which the people believing, everyone gives money according to their ability. The priest takes the money, and putting it into some dishes, sets them upon the top of their low flat-roofed houses, and falls to invocating their God to come and receive it, which with a many loud hallows and outcries, knocking the ground with sticks, and beating themselves, is performed by the priest, and seconded by the people.
>
> After they have thus a while wearied themselves, the priest by his conjuration brings in a devil amongst them, in the shape sometimes of a fowl, sometimes of a beast, and sometimes of a man, at which the people being amazed, not daring to stir, he improves the opportunity, steps out, and makes sure of the money, and then returns to lay the spirit, who in the meantime is sometimes gone, and takes some of the company along with him: but if any *English* at such times do come among them, it puts a period to their succeeding, and they will desire their absence, telling them their God will not come whilst they are there.[17]

Earlier students seem to have agreed that the Algonkian tribes of the Hudson River observed a green corn festival. Ruttenber said merely: "The Harvest moon, or the new moon in August, they also honored with a feast, in acknowledgement

---

[17] Denton, 1937, pp. 8-9.

of the product of their fields and their success in the chase."[18] Alanson Skinner remarked:

> The religion of the Indians was marked by periodic ceremonies, one of which has come down to the present day among the modern remnants of the Shinnecock of Long Island and the Mohegan of Connecticut. This is the June Meeting, which was formerly a ceremony held for the green corn. The Delaware in Oklahoma and Canada still perform a number of other annual ceremonies.[19]

The "June meeting" was held on Long Island, but not in Connecticut.

Nevertheless, there is but slight evidence of such rituals among the tribes of the upper and lower Hudson. Wassenaer, writing about 1624, gave some notes on the Indians of New Netherlands and a brief account of their ceremonialism, apparently including all of the tribes of the Hudson in his description. Especially, he noted the midwinter and green corn festivals: "They allow the succeeding moons to appear without any feasting (that is, since the winter festival); but they celebrate the new August moon by another festival, as their harvest then approaches."[20]

THE DELAWARE AND SOUTHEASTERN ALGONKIANS

THE various dispersed bands of Delaware in Canada, Oklahoma, and other localities have carried on their green corn festivals almost to the present day, but recent accounts are not as thorough as might be desired and are difficult to correlate with earlier historical data. It is often considered that Delaware ceremonialism has been deeply affected by Iroquois influence; yet a better knowledge of the rituals and traditions of both the Lenape and of the peoples of southern New England might demonstrate closer relations between these two areas than between the peoples of either area and the Iroquois. It is believed that available data on green corn ceremonies of the

---

[18] Ruttenber, 1872, pp. 28–29. [19] Skinner, 1915a, p. 10.
[20] Wassenaer, 1850, p. 29.

various eastern Algonkian peoples may show such basic similarities. Comparison of the older Lenape data with the recent ethnological data from various Delaware communities may throw light on older practices and also help to explain some of our New England material.

William Penn, in the summer of 1683, witnessed what was apparently a Lenape festival in Pennsylvania and recorded some details in a published "letter." The whole account is worth quoting:

> Their worship consists of two parts, sacrifice and cantico. Their sacrifice is their first fruits. The first and fattest buck they kill, goeth to the fire, where he is all burnt, with a mournful ditty of him who performeth the ceremony, but with such marvellous fervency and labor of body, that he will even sweat to a foam. The other part is their cantico, performed by round dances, sometimes words, sometimes songs, then shouts; two being in the middle who begin, and by singing and drumming on a board, direct the chorus. Their postures in the dance are very antic and differing, but all keep measure. This is done with equal earnestness and labor, but great appearance of joy. In the fall, when the corn cometh in, they begin to feast one another. There have been two great feastivals already, to which all come that will. I was at one myself. Their entertainment was a great seat by a spring under some shady trees, and twenty bucks, with hot cakes of new corn, both wheat and beans, which they make up in a square form, in the leaves of the stem, and bake them in the ashes, and after that they fall to dance. But they who go must carry a small present in their money; it may be sixpence, which is made of the bone of a fish; the black with them is as gold; the white silver; they call it wampum.[21]

Gabriel Thomas, in 1608, said of the Delaware:

> They observe new moons, they offer their first fruits to a Maneto, or suppos'd Deity, whereof they have two, one as they fansie, above (good) another below (bad).[22]

John Brickell, who was carried to Ohio in 1791 by the Delaware and who stayed with them near Sandusky until 1795,

---

[21] Penn, 1862, pp. 233–34.   [22] Thomas, 1900, 5: 7.

indicated that a green corn ceremony preceded the first seasonal use of the new corn:

> They have their regular feasts, such as the first corn that is fit to use is made a feast offering; and when they start on a hunting expedition, the first game that is taken they skin and dress whole, breaking not a bone, leaving on the head, ears and hoofs.[23]

John Wampum (Chief Waubuno), writing in the latter part of the nineteenth century, remarked: "They keep annual feasts.... A feast of the first fruits which they do not permit themselves to taste until they have made an offering of them to the manitu oo al, or gods...."[24]

In the major early Delaware sources, usable material on Delaware ritual is surprisingly sparse. Loskiel gave only the most generalized account,[25] and Heckwelder only added some notes to Loskiel's account without clarifying any of it.[26] Zeisberger gave a general account of what would appear to be an artificial synthesis in which he has mixed elements of a number of different rituals, and said: "There are four or five kinds of feasts, the ceremonies of which differ much from one another."[27] His account was incorporated into Loskiel's description of Delaware ritualism.

Loskiel described several types of rituals, only a few of which are tentatively identifiable and spoke in very general terms of feasts, by which he seems to mean nonperiodic feasts given by private households for special purposes. He differentiated sacrifices, which apparently are parts of various rituals, and overlooked the seasonal periodicity of certain rites, the green corn festival and the big house ceremony included, confusing them in his account with other rituals which are nondistinctive. It is well to remember, however, that Loskiel had no direct contact with the Indians he described and had all of his data at second hand, from the accounts of other Moravian mission-

[23] Brickell, 1844, p. 49.   [24] Waubuno, p. 27.
[25] Loskiel, 1794, pp. 33–47.   [26] Heckwelder, 1876, pp. 208–14.
[27] Zeisberger, 1910, p. 137.

aries in America. One remark may apply to a corn ceremonial: "To Indian corn they sacrifice bears' flesh, but to deer and bears, Indian corn."[28]

Heckwelder, despite his many years of residence among these Indians, did not attempt to improve on Loskiel. In view of the confusion in all three of these Moravians' works, it is questionable whether they had any but the most superficial knowledge of their Indian parishioners, despite their knowledge of the Delaware language. It is known from early and contemporary sources that the Delaware actually clung to their native religion with the utmost tenacity and that these rituals survived the Moravian missionaries, yet these historians have certainly left a meager record of Delaware ceremonialism. Mrs. Jameson, who visited the Moravian Delaware at Thames, Ontario, Canada (the present Moraviantown), about 1835, gave a surprising insight into the actual extent of Christianization of these people:

> The Moravian missionary admitted that only a small portion of the tribe under his care and tuition could be called Christians. There were about two hundred and thirty baptized out of seven hundred, principally women and children, and yet the mission had been established and supported for more than a century. Their only chance, he said was with the children; and on my putting the question to him in a direct form, he replied decidedly, that he considered the civilization and conversion of the Indian, *to any great extent*, a hopeless task.[29]

F. G. Speck, in his recent studies of Oklahoma Delaware religion,[30] discovered that the green corn festival (xaskwi'·mi· laᵃkeyɔ'k'an, "corn ceremony") had not been performed in the lifetime of his informants. Traditional accounts, derived from their parents who had witnessed this observance, make it possible to venture some statements about this ritual. The rite was announced in advance by two masked messengers wearing corn-husk clothing, who rode about demanding a trifling contribution from each person that they met. If refused,

[28] Loskiel, 1794, p. 40.   [29] Jameson, 1839, 2: 40.
[30] Speck, 1937, pp. 79–90.

they smeared excrement upon the person as a punishment, this preliminary rite being called we 'muiha'ləwe·s ("excrement daubing"). These messengers were also the dance leaders at the festival which was held a week or so later and at which they used at least two special masks.

The feast itself was opened with an address by a speaker chosen for the occasion and a series of traditional dances for the earlier part of the day. Men's dances led by the masked messengers alternated with women's dances, the leaders of which were not masked. A feast, with corn bread and hominy, followed, and an all-night series of social (mixed) dances concluded the observance.

The use of corn foods, with prayers for the propitiation of the Corn Mother, was emphasized. The dance had to continue until morning. It is said that this ceremony originated in a time when the corn had been offended and had left the people, the green corn ceremony beginning as a device to plead with the Corn Mother for the return of the maize to the people. This ceremony was addressed to the Creator and the Corn Mother, the dances were accompanied by rattles and drums, and the ceremony was held outdoors on a prepared piece of ground.[31]

Alanson Skinner has carelessly equated such rituals as the green corn festival with the big house ritual. After giving a brief outline of the Oklahoma Delaware big house ritual, he said:

Such are the old-time ceremonies as they are tenaciously preserved by the survivors of the old New York Delawares. Even the degenerate remnant of the Mohegan in Connecticut have a pathetic survival of the olden times in their "Green Corn Dance," which has now become a sort of church fair. The Shinnecocks and the Montauks of Long Island still hold a "June Meeting," which is but a pitiful memory of some ancient ceremony that was no doubt like the annual ceremony of the Delawares.[32]

M. R. Harrington, in his extensive study of Oklahoma

[31] *Ibid.*, p. 26 (chart). [32] Skinner, 1915*b*, p. 55.

Delaware ritual, apparently found little evidence of green corn ceremonialism, for he has included no data pertaining to such a festival in his published accounts. According to the protagonist of his book, *Dickon Among the Lenape:*

> Green corn time was always a happy time in Lenape land, with much feasting; yet I never saw a public dance to celebrate the occasion, as I hear is the custom among many other tribes. Of each kind of First Fruits, however, a little was offered to the man-it-to-wuk, or unseen powers.[33]

Speck, in his recent study of the Munsee-Mahican big house which functioned at Smoothtown, Six Nations Reserve, Ontario, Canada, until about 1850, included a good account of the green corn festival as known from the tradition of his oldest informants. This ceremony was held in the big house and included many of the features noted for the winter big house ceremony. It was held in September, Xwathkwi·' mkan ki' coX ("corn beginning to ripen month"):

> In the September phase of the new moon, usually late in the period, the Green Corn Ceremony was performed. Lasting for seven days and nights, it was a harvest ceremony in a broad sense with reference to the maturing of beans and other crops as well as corn. Terminating the agricultural activities of the year and being therefore considered as the ritual only second in importance to the Bear Sacrifice Ceremony occurring about six months later, it introduced the hunting season. Its rites included about the same repertoire as the Bear Sacrifice Ceremony, but were distinguished by a substitution of corn-husk false face dancers for the wooden false face dancers of the other. The ceremony, opening with a prayer and sermon by the chief on the afternoon of the first day, began with the dance of the corn-husk mask company. Three men wearing corn-husk masks and naked except for breech-cloth, led by another man without mask but with a long staff, entered each door of the Big House. They converged upon the center-post in crawling motions which "swept" the floor of the sanctuary and purged it from evil influences, especially disease. Each standing in his own place, not circling around, they performed a dance at the center-post.

[33] Harrington, 1938, p. 55.

The second event on the program was another sermon by the chief. Then followed the Men's Dance, the dancers being either naked or in full costume. The mixed dance followed this, then the Woman's Dance. In succession the Nighthawk Dance, the Robin Dance, and the Raccoon Dance followed these. The night's celebration was terminated with a sermon by the chief.

The same order of performance was the rule for seven days and nights. On the last night of the ceremony just before sunrise the women performed a procession around the center-post and left the Big House by the west door. They passed around the south side of the building toward the east door. Here the men are waiting. As they passed the men, they held aloft a cake which was grabbed for by the men until the supply was exhausted. Then all of those who took part entered the Big House through the east door and took their places. The chief of the band gave another sermon, terminating the ceremony.[34]

Several features in this account are worthy of note. The nighthawk dance is probably the equivalent of the widely performed eagle dance, but in no other instance is the eagle dance a part of the green corn ceremony. This is also the only modern account in which the center post is mentioned as utilized in this ritual, but there are parallels in older Creek, Cherokee, and Natchez accounts which will be discussed later. The all-night duration of the dancing and the morning greeting of the sunrise are significant and widely distributed traits which will be discussed later.

The Algonkian tribes of the Virginia area observed some sort of festival when the green corn was mature enough for eating, but there is almost no information about the content or function of such a ritual. John Smith, in 1624, made vague reference to harvest observances:

> From September until the midst of November are the chief feasts and sacrifice. Then have they plentie of fruits as well planted as natural, as corne, greene and ripe, fish, fowle, and wilde beastes exceeding fat.[35]
>
> It could not be perceived that they keepe any day as more holy

[34] Speck, 1945, p. 31.   [35] Smith, 1907, I: 58.

than another: But only in some great distress of want, feare of enemies, trains of triumph and gathering together their fruits, the whole company of men, women, and children come together to solemnities.[36]

Thomas Grover referred to a similar ritualism:

They offer the First fruits of all things; the first *Deer* they kill after they are in season, they lay privately on the head of a Tree near the place where they killed it, and they say, no good luck will befall them that year if they do not offer the first of everything.[37]

Robert Beverley gave a more complete but rather fanciful account of a first fruits ceremony:

They use many Divinations and Enchantments, and frequently offer Burnt Sacrifices to the Evil Spirit. The people annually present their first Fruits of every Season and Kind, namely, of Birds, Beasts, Fish, Fruits, Plants, Roots, and of all other things, which they esteem either of Profit or Pleasure to Themselves. They repeat their Offerings as frequently as they have great success in their Wars, or their Fishing, Fowling or Hunting.[38]

I never could learn that they had any certain time or set days for their Solemnities: but they have appointed Feasts that happen according to the several seasons. They solemnize a day for the plentiful coming of their Wild Fowl, such as Geese, Ducks, Teal, etc. for the returns of their Hunting Seasons, and for the ripening of certain Fruits: but the greatest Annual Feast they have, is at the time of the corn gathering, at which they revel several days together. To these they universally contribute, as they do to the gathering in the Corn. On this occasion they have their greatest variety of Pastimes, and more especially of their War-Dances, and Heroick Songs; in which they boast that their Corn being now gathered, they have store enough for their Women and Children; and have nothing to do, but to go to War, Travel, and to seek out for New Adventures.[39]

Beverley seems to have been the last observer to record so much as a note on these ceremonies, and thus there is but a mere suggestion of the significance of a green corn festival. F. G.

---

[36] *Ibid.*, p. 74.   [37] Grover, 1904, p. 24.
[38] Beverley, 1705, 3: 34.   [39] *Ibid.*, p. 43.

Speck, in a general account of the culture of the Powhatan tribes, drew some conclusions from the data then available:

> In the North Carolina sub-group we have strong indications, from the illustrations of White, of what is evidently Muskogian influence in the ceremony of the corn harvest (the "busk" of the Creek) with its ceremonial adjuncts, the emetic of "black drink," the scratching rite, and other details. Except that in White's pictures the people of Secotan are seated in a circle instead of in the "square" ground of the southeastern tribes, we might imagine the procedure to be a Muskogean one.[40]

A. H. Keane had previously equated White's dance scenes with the Iroquois green corn festival.[41] Unfortunately, there are no features indicated in White's drawings which are diagnostic of any particular ceremony or indicative of any special direction of influence, in the light of present data, and it would seem impossible to decide which, if any, of White's drawings might refer to a green corn ceremony.[42]

Certain traits in the green corn ceremonies of the Algonkian speaking peoples seem significant. First of these is the sacrifice element. In Roger Williams' Narraganset account, presents of all sorts are given away to the participants; in Denton's Long Island account, wampum is collected and presented, apparently to some deity; in Speck's account of the modern Mohegan meeting, the proceeds from the sale of handicrafts are given to the church; in Penn's Lenape account, wampum is brought as a present to the festival; in Speck's Oklahoma Delaware account, the masked messengers who notify the people demand presents. Nothing is known of the method of disposal of these presents at the green corn festivals, but their use for the ceremonial payment of major participants in the big house ceremony of various Delaware communities has been noted. This sacrifice element is reminiscent of the Iroquois collection of food for the longhouse feasts, of tobacco for the sacrifices, and of wampum and ribbons for the decoration of

---

[40] Speck, 1924, p. 193.

[41] Keane, in preface to Frobenius, 1909, p. viii.

[42] Three variant sets of these plates were consulted, as follows: Beverley, 1705; White, n.d.; and Hariot, 1895.

the sacrificed white dog in the midwinter ceremony, and especially of the wagers for the great bowl game. The ideal of sacrifice is especially noteworthy in the Iroquois bowl game, which is closely associated with the Iroquois green corn festival, but the Algonkian peoples do not seem to have used the dice game in any similar ceremonial association. This sacrifice motif is not recorded for the southeastern Algonkians.

The bark-covered longhouse, best known as an Iroquois ceremonial structure associated with the green corn as well as other festivals, is specifically associated with the Narraganset green corn festival in the accounts both of Roger Williams and of Ninegrat. The survival of the Mohegan ceremonial structure was a longhouse-like bower, perhaps similar to structures associated with various summer ceremonies in other parts of southern New England. The Smoothtown band of Munsee-Mahican held their green corn festival in the big house, but according to Penn's account and Speck's Oklahoma Delaware account the ceremony was held outdoors on a prepared ground. Other writers are silent on this point. Only in Speck's Smoothtown account is there any mention of a centerpost and its function in the Delaware ceremony. The rectangular longhouse seems to be replaced by a rectangular square ground as one goes south, a matter of some significance in the comparison of southeastern ceremonial grounds with the structures of the Northeast. The Shawnee ceremonial structure is described as a rectangular, pine-bark covered structure,[43] but there are no data on green corn ceremonies.

The Iroquois and Delaware ceremonial structures are replete with direction and world symbolism, but no data on this point are extant from New England. The Narraganset longhouse seems to have been specific for the green corn festival and may have carried similar interpretations. It is possible that the Narraganset preserved an older order of things and that the Iroquois and Delaware longhouses originally associated with the green corn festival were later transferred to additional associations. The Delaware structure survived to serve gener-

[43] Hawkins, 1848, p. 41; 1916, p. 63.

ally for winter ceremonies, and the southeastern square ground may have originally been a house structure.

THE IROQUOIS

AMONG the existing Iroquois groups which preserve a pattern of aboriginal ceremonialism, two rituals are most prominent. The midwinter festival, generally held in late January, marks the beginning of the Iroquois ceremonial and economic year, and the green corn festival, in August, is held when the new corn is first abundantly available. The great significance of these two ceremonies is indicated by the precept of Handsome Lake that all children must be formally given names before the green corn and midwinter festivals, although most of the longhouses bestow names during these functions. At Allegany Reservation the day before the beginning of the ceremonies is set aside for naming children.[44]

A basic concept of Iroquois ceremonialism is the thanksgiving function of ritual; each ceremonial observance is intended to thank the Creator and his agents for certain phases of the world structure from which all the benefits of man are derived, as a result of his position in this structure and his relationship to all the other members and parts of it. As a secondary objective each ceremony is intended to honor and propitiate both the Creator and specific features of the world which he has set up, thus making more probable the continuation of man's benefit from the proper functioning of the various members and agents of this universe. The midwinter festival marks the beginning of the new Iroquois year. It is a period of meditation and thanksgiving for all the benefits of the previous year, and of prayer for similar blessings in the new year. In this ritual man's essential relationship to the rest of the universe is defined and proclaimed, and whatever strains this relationship has been subjected to in the past year are patched and healed. It is probably due to this concept that such features as the dream guessing and the procedures of medicine societies have become important in this special ceremonial association.

[44] Fenton, 1936, p. 10.

The universality of the midwinter festival is sufficient cause for its position as the most important Iroquois ritual. Flannery's suggestion as to the recency of the great importance of this ceremony is certainly highly conjectural: "Apparently the Festival of Dream Fulfillment '(Midwinter Festival)' was so emphasized among the Huron-Iroquois, at the beginning of the 17th century, that the corn festival had faded into the background."[45]

The green corn festival, the culmination of a series of rituals directly concerned with the planting and growth of cultivated crops, is held when the unripe corn is available as food and is primarily concerned with returning thanks for the gifts of agriculture and with prayer and propitiation that this good fortune may extend into the future and that winter will not arrive until crops are in. There seem to be no references to a green corn ceremony prior to the early nineteenth century, unless Lalemant's statements concerning the Huron of the seventeenth century may have been occasioned by such a festival.[46]

Lewis Morgan witnessed this ritual in 1846 and published a good description of it in 1851.[47] He gave the wrong name for the ceremony, but noted the occurrence of the four sacred ceremonies in the content and discussed the ideological background of the ceremony, noting the significance of the "Three Sisters" (corn, beans, and squash). In the century following Morgan's publication, one finds abundant references to the Iroquois green corn festival but no thorough study of the ceremony until the past decade, when Arthur C. Parker, J. N. B. Hewitt, F. G. Speck, and William N. Fenton began to study the ceremonial cycles of various Iroquois communities.

Fenton[48] seems to have first discovered the structural unity of the green corn festival as a recurring part of the midwinter festival and the reappearance of the procedures of a single day of the green corn festival in yet other festivals:

The Green Corn Festival marks the middle of the year. When

[45] Flannery, 1939, p. 134.　[46] Lalemant, 1898*a*, p. 53; 1898*b*, p. 81.
[47] Morgan, 1851, pp. 196–205.　[48] Fenton, 1936.

the corn is ready to eat, late in August or early September, the Faith-keepers gather the community to the Longhouse to name children born since the Seneca New Year. The festival lasts four mornings until noon, including the preliminary day to name the children. The women's song (tǫwı'sas) occurs on the fourth afternoon, after the Bowl Game. Identical in form with the later three days of the midwinter ritual, which are devoted to the Four Sacred Ceremonies, the Green Corn Festival may extend beyond the minimal number of days, before one moiety defeats the other in the bowl game. Then a social dance must be held every evening before the game until it is finished. The Green Corn Festival returns thanks to all the spirit-forces. It is especially for the vegetables and fruits which have ripened during the season. The Creator and his Appointed ones are thanked that the crops planted in spring have reached fruition, and he is remembered for life, health, and sustenance during the past six months. It is hoped that the winter will not be too severe, and will not approach until they have gathered in their crops and have gone hunting.[49]

The Seventh day (of the Midwinter Festival) marks the celebration of the Great Feather Dance, which is the first of four ceremonies left by the Creator for the people to enjoy, and later confirmed by Handsome Lake. Since the ceremonies performed on this day comprise the external form of the Planting, Strawberry, second day of the Green Corn (i.e., first day of the ritual proper, after naming of children), and the Harvest Festivals, I will describe them below in some detail. In brief, they consist of a first Feather Dance for the Faith-keepers, the Women's Dance, an intermission for changing adult names, installing new Faith-keepers, or appointing their moiety reciprocates, which occurs only at the New Year and Green Corn, and the final Great Feather Dance.

The eighth day is identical in form with the third day of the Green Corn. It consists of: a tobacco burning invocation to the Creator, which was once used over the white dog; a rite of personal thanksgiving and singing a Personal Chant (adǫ́·wę?), which is the second of the four ceremonies, for chiefs, headmen, Faith-keepers and common gentry, ending with Handsome Lake's version; and the performance of the Thanksgiving Dance, the third ceremony, in which a priest, holding a miniature bow, intersperses the songs with fourteen prayers of thanks to the Creator for the things he prayed for in the tobacco invocation. Coldspring alone celebrates the Personal Chant and

[49] *Ibid.*, p. 9.

Thanksgiving Dance on the same day. The evening is devoted to a social dance, which opens and closes with a brief Feather Dance. ... The moieties separate for the bowl game.

The ninth day should terminate the festival if one moiety wins all 102 beans (in the Bowl Game) from its cousins before noon. One moiety is previously selected to represent the Creator, and the game of bowl and counters, which is the fourth ceremony, epitomizes the struggle of the good brother over his evil twin for the control of the earth, as described in the origin legend. The women celebrate their rite (tǫwıʻsas) in the afternoon, giving thanks for the crops and begging for their return in the spring. It corresponds to adǫ'wę? for the men. If the bowl game is not finished on the first morning, as is frequently the case, a social dance is held every evening until someone wins the game on a following morning. That ends the festival. Then all are freed of their responsibilities and sent back to their daily tasks.[50]

Fenton has kindly made available his notes on the green corn festival at Coldspring longhouse, Allegany Reservation, New York, and I give here a synopsis of this ceremony, as performed in 1933 and 1934. The preliminary wampum confession rite is held a week or ten days before the green corn festival, this being the purifying ritual of the Handsome Lake religion. A second wampum confession ritual occurs several days later. At this meeting the date for the green corn festival is announced,[51] and the speakers and officials for the festival are appointed:

The confession rite, which should precede all festivals addressed to the Creator, is an opportunity for the community to prepare itself for the coming celebration and has some claim to antiquity.[52]

The first day of the green corn festival at Allegany is not properly a part of the festival, but is a preliminary day set aside for the naming of children. A general thanksgiving to all the spirit forces (ganǫ'·nyǫk), a great feather dance for the faithkeepers, the naming of children, the regular great feather dance (ʔostówä?go·wa·), and a feast are the chief events of this day.

[50] *Ibid.*, p. 13.   [51] Fenton, MS *a*.   [52] Fenton, 1936, p. 16.

The second day (September 5, 1933; August 28, 1934) is the first day of the green corn festival proper, the first day of the hęnondekwe·s ("gathering the crops"). On this day the preliminary announcements to the people are followed by the announcement of the good health of the settlement, a thanksgiving address (ganǫ'·nyǫk), and the first part of the feather dance for the faithkeepers (similar to that of the first day). This is followed by the women's dance, dedicated to the agricultural plants, the ʔęskänyeʔ·gainǫgáyǫka·ʔ("women's dance, old time song"), in which the women carry ears of corn. After this follows the ritual for changing adult names, then the first of the four sacred ceremonies, the great feather dance (ʔostoweʔ-go·wa ganonyowáneh) in costume, and the final announcements, thanks to participants, assignment of the next day's duties, and the feast,[53] concluding about noon:

The program on this day recurs five times; the seventh day of the Midwinter Festival, the Planting Festival, the Strawberry Festival, the second day of the Green Corn, and the Harvest Festivals. This day exhibits the ritual pattern which underlies all of the Seneca Ceremonies.[54]

The Traditional Women's Dance (ʔęsägnyeʔ·gainǫgáyǫka·ʔ) returns thanks only to the (three) sisters, Our-life-supporters (dowę'·nondę'nonde·djǫhéhgo)—the corn, the beans, and the squash—which are on the earth.[55]

The third day begins with the collection of tobacco and food from the various households and with the usual chores at the cookhouse and longhouse. The usual announcements and thanksgivings follow, and the tobacco burning invocation, as described previously, is conducted. Then the men's adǫ·węʔ are sung, this being the second sacred ceremony, followed by the thanksgiving dance, ganeǫwo, the third sacred ceremony. This is followed by the usual thanksgivings and a feast, which is concluded a little after noon. This day's ritual corresponds to that of the eighth day of the midwinter festival.[56]

[53] Fenton, MSa. [54] Fenton, 1936, p. 14. [55] *Ibid.*, p. 17.
[56] Fenton, MSa.

The personal chant is composed of individual thanksgiving for one's wife, one's family, or the life of a friend, and the singing of one of many songs which are to some extent the property of one family and possibly of the clan. It is the last song sung by a warrior[57] before death:

The tobacco invocation, formerly over the white dog, is addressed to the Creator. It contains the most elaborate references to the duties of the appointed-ones to the people. It is performed twice a year, but less elaborately in the summer.[58]

The Thanksgiving or Harvest Dance is a costumed dance for men and women, which is interspersed by fourteen thanksgiving chants by a priest, who addresses the several groups of spirit-forces.[59]

The ninth day is dedicated to two separate ceremonial observances. The great bowl game is held in the morning, preceded by collection of wagers and must be finished at noon, to be resumed on the following morning[60] if necessary:

The Great Bowl Game or wager, symbolizes the struggle of the good brother, the Creator, with his evil twin brother for the control of the earth. The town divides spatially into moieties which exchange the role of playing for the Creator from Green Corn to New Year.[61]

In the afternoon the women meet in the longhouse to hold their thanksgiving rite (tǫwi'sas), which returns thanks to the life supporters (vegetable crops) and is the equivalent of the men's adǫ·we?. First, the women's songs are sung to the sound of rattles and of broom handles struck on the floor (like pestles). The men interrupt these songs with their adǫ·we? and then join them in the round dance, now singing for the corn. This day's ritual corresponds exactly with that of the ninth day of the midwinter festival at Allegany.[62] The tǫwi'sas rite seems to correspond to the linking arms dance, a social dance, and its relationships are discussed later:

The women's song corresponds to the Personal Chant for men, and

[57] Fenton, 1936, p. 16. [58] *Ibid.*, p. 16. [59] *Ibid.*, p. 16.
[60] Fenton, MS*a*. [61] Fenton, 1936, p. 16. [62] Fenton, MS*a*.

embraces all the Appointed-ones from food on earth through the middle pantheon to the Creator.[63]

The afternoon of the women's thanksgiving rite is followed by a series of social dances in the evening:

The Creator's evil brother is credited with social dances, which he intended as his Sacred Ceremonies. Devil Dance (his Feather Dance), Grinding-an-arrow (Harvest Dance), and the Linking-arms Dance, sometimes called Bean (Traditional Women's Dance), were frowned upon by Handsome Lake. The latter was the only dance permitting physical contact between sexes. It is now frequently performed in single file, sometimes using the ancient songs which ridicule a youth's devotion to an older woman with bumps on her forehead.[64]

The social dance equivalents may reflect a more ancient ceremonial usage of the features which Handsome Lake condemned. In particular, the linking-arms dance and the women's thanksgiving rite suggest a Cherokee parallel, the so-called green corn dance, ani'tikwɔleluhuska'hi ("they have bumps on their foreheads"), which will be discussed elsewhere in this study. The tǫwi'sas, according to an origin tale collected by Jeremiah Curtin, was introduced by captives who escaped from the Cherokee.[65]

The green corn ceremony as described for Allegany Reservation may be representative of this Iroquois ceremony, but variations occur in each locality:

All of the Iroquois longhouses share the Four Sacred Ceremonies. They are: Feather Dance, Personal Chant, the Harvest or Thanksgiving Dance, and the Bowl Game. Nevertheless, the sequence of performances differs from group to group. At Coldspring for the last three days of both the Midwinter and Green Corn Festivals, the order is Feather Dance, Personal Chant, and Harvest Dance on the same day, with the Bowl Game last. Coldspring is alone in celebrating the second and third of the ceremonies on the same day. At Newtown and Plank Road the Feather Dance and Harvest or Thanksgiving Dance come on the same day, at Tonawanda the Personal Chant and the

[63] Fenton, 1936, p. 16. [64] *Ibid.*, p. 18.
[65] Mooney, 1900, pp. 265–367.

Bowl Game come together on the last day of the New Year Festival, but separately on the third and fourth days of the Green Corn.[66]

The modern Green Corn Dance at Tonawanda longhouse has undergone a change since Morgan's observation (circa 1850). Now, the festival lasts two mornings, and a third night is dedicated to Our-life-supporters since they grow only at night. The Bowl Game and Personal Chant occur on the second morning.[67]

At Newtown longhouse the bowl game occurs on the third day, but the women's thanksgiving rite is held on the afternoon of the following day, with the social dances on the evening of the fourth day.[68]

Despite these local differences, some of which are still evolving, the same major outline seems to underlie the green corn festival and the last three days of the midwinter festival at all of the longhouses for which there is adequate data.[69] The underlying concepts of thanksgiving are dominant everywhere, and the major significance of the green corn festival in the ceremonial cycle of each Iroquois community is apparent. It seems probable that either the green corn festival procedure was incorporated into the midwinter festival and that changes in both have been kept parallel by conscious efforts of the Iroquois, or that the present duplication is the result of a revamping of Iroquois ceremonialism at some time in the past. The green corn festival is a major and integral part of the yearly cycle of ritual observances, and can hardly be considered a recent development. The revelation of Handsome Lake, the Seneca prophet, occurring before 1800, pushed many specific features of less importance out of the ceremonies proper into the associated groups of social dances; this revelation sharply defined ceremonial observances. The influence of the Handsome Lake religion has not been sufficient to suppress entirely the features it condemned, and it seems to have only strengthened the place of the major and central ceremonial features which Handsome Lake respected and upheld. The

---

[66] Fenton, 1936, p. 21.   [67] *Ibid.*, p. 21 (footnote).   [68] Fenton, MS*b*.
[69] Fenton, 1936, 1941, and MS*c*; Morgan, 1851; Witthoft, 1946*a*; Parker, 1912; Speck, MS*b*.

structural pattern of Iroquois ceremonialism seems to be older than Handsome Lake's influence and is probably a principle which Handsome Lake understood and recommended. It represents an existing functional pattern which he tried to perpetuate, to judge by his precepts regarding the four sacred ceremonies and the various ritual sequences.[70]

The sparsity of material relating to green corn ceremonies from the various Algonkian areas has already been noted, especially in the older and standard historical sources, yet there are sufficient data from those areas to indicate the existence of such rituals. The Iroquois are the only group in the Northeast for which there is any body of modern ethnological data pertaining to green corn ceremonialism, yet there seems to be nothing in the extensive early literature which refers to such a ceremony. The ethnologist, proceeding only from his data, might conclude that such a ceremony is Iroquoian, and that any remnants of such ritualism among modern Algonkian peoples would be due to Iroquoian influence. The historian might conclude that the Algonkian peoples could have had minor ceremonies devoted to the green corn, but that such rituals were unknown among the Iroquois; if familiar with modern ethnographic material, he would possibly conclude that most of it was a modern fabrication on the part of the Iroquois. It would seem probable that peoples of both stocks had a major ritual concerned with the availability of the new corn and that each group may have evolved specializations in the function and content of this ritual.

Probably not much more will ever be known about it, because the ethnological sources in most of the area are destroyed. A continued study of the whole of Iroquois ceremonialism may sometime permit a more thorough knowledge of one part of this large territory, but progress even in that area will come to a halt with the end of the various Iroquoian communities. From the historian's data one can hope for little knowledge of the actual life of the people; every reference is a mere puzzle to be explained or discarded through observation of the existing

[70] Parker, 1913, pp. 40–42; Morgan, 1851, pp. 242–44.

ethnic reality. The accounts of early observers, who overlooked what is now known to be the most significant objective aspects of Indian religion, certainly can give no useable picture of aboriginal life; they furnish only footnotes and occasional documentation on the more spectacular incidents which may have attracted their attention. Such material, however, is considered a final check on the field data of the ethnologist; the value of an account is believed to increase with its age; history is considered necessary to give credibility to modern objective accounts. One can gain abundant footnotes from the early accounts, and one can even synthesize them into a sizable description of what appears to be a sketch of a culture, but attempts to study one particular feature as it is noted in the older sources, rather than to collect a hodgepodge of assorted curious details, may soon come to an end because of inadequate data.

An ethnological investigator among any of the existing eastern tribes finds that the clergy, storekeepers, agents, and other white people who are in close contact with Indians actually know and care very little about Indian culture, unless, as rarely occurs, they have also become students of this subject. He prefers to put no faith in their accounts, but classes them as another ethnic factor interesting because of their functions, not because of their knowledge. The so-called "White Cherokee," white people who live with the Eastern Cherokee, who have been raised on a reservation and who often speak Cherokee, are conspicuous examples of persons ignorant of almost everything Indian. The ethnologist, however, is expected to pay lip service to the written accounts of earlier representatives of the whites who stood in similar relationship to Indian cultures, on the general assumption that proximity results in knowledge and culture transference, a misconception to which white neighbors of Indians have always adhered. Anyone who has attempted to understand Iroquoian institutions in terms of both the ethnological picture and the early accounts is probably conscious of the huge gap in understanding and observation between Indian and European cultures. In order to interpret the *Jesuit Relations* properly, one might have to study not only the existing Iroquois communities but also existing Jesuit communities. Then he could accurately weigh and evaluate these authors' knowledge and understanding of the peoples with whom they were acquainted, provided that he also considered the public for whom they wrote, and the distortions and selectivity that were introduced into their writings by the demands of their market. Both historical accounts and ethnographic data should be utilized with some consideration of the shortcomings which may be found in both bodies of information, and with some attention to acculturation and recent culture history.

THE CHEROKEE

THE Cherokee, perhaps more than any other Indian group in the eastern United States, responded to the efforts of the missionary and teacher with a strong desire to become responsible and enlightened participants in the culture of their white neighbors. This hope was frustrated by their forcible removal to the West in 1838, although this incident did not result in a reaction against acculturation. Only the Cherokee who lived farthest from white communities, the so-called "Mountain Indians," seem to have resisted the impact of European culture at all effectively. James Mooney, earliest student of Cherokee ethnology, formed some definite opinions about the destruction of Cherokee culture:

> For many years the hunter and warrior had given place to the farmer and mechanic, and the forced expatriation made the change complete and final. Torn from their native streams and mountains, their council house fires extinguished and their townhouses burned behind them, and transported bodily to a far distant country where everything was new and strange, they were obliged perforce to forego the old life and adjust themselves to changed surroundings. The ball play was neglected and the green-corn dance proscribed, while the heroic tradition of former days became a fading memory or a tale to amuse a child.[71]

[71] Mooney, 1900, p. 146.

Only the "ignorant mountain people" (as they were described by Armstrong, an agent in Indian Territory about 1842)[72] seem to have been able to conserve much of their aboriginal culture, and even these remnants seem to be on the same road their less marginal neighbors had previously chosen. One group, the Cherokee of Qualla Reservation, still emain in their original habitat and constitute the best field for Cherokee ethnography; another, the group noted by Armstrong in Indian Territory, form a conservative group in Oklahoma today. It is not surprising that almost all data on green corn ceremonialism come from the Qualla Reservation, and that data from all available sources vary considerably and give evidence of drastic change in the past two centuries.

Charles Hicks, a mixed blood Cherokee chief of the early nineteenth century, has left a brief notice concerning the Cherokee green corn festival and related observances, written for the Reverend Hoyt of the American Board of Missions in 1817-18 and published in the Raleigh *Register:*

Before eating the green corn when in the milk, the people collect in the different towns and villages at night, when the ——— (not understood in Mr. Hicks' original) comes, the conjuror takes some of the grains of seven ears of corn and feeds the fire, i.e. burns them. After this each family is allowed to cook and eat their roasting-ears, but not before they drink a tea of wild horehound. In like manner they observe the same custom before eating the bean when it fills in the hull.

The green corn dance, so called, has been highly esteemed formerly. This is held when the corn is getting hard, and lasts four days, and when the national council sits—a quantity of venison being procured to supply the dance. It is said that a person was formerly chosen to speak to the people on each day in a language that is partly lost—at least there is very little of it known now. At such times as the above, a piece of land is laid off and persons appointed to occupy it—no others being allowed to use it while the feast continues.[73]

A paraphrase of this account is included in an 1833 mission tract:

[72] Schoolcraft, 1858, 6: 531.   [73] Hicks, 1818.

Cornelia. Indian conjurers are generally called *medicine men*, and rank next to the chiefs. They are consulted with great ceremony, by all descriptions of persons, and are accounted to be very powerful; formerly, there were annual festivals, in which the conjurers bore a very conspicuous part.

Delia. Please to describe some of their festivals.

Cornelia. They used to have one when the corn was in the milk, before they tasted it; on these occasions, there was a general meeting of all the inhabitants of the district or village, and, after all were assembled, the conjuror took the kernels from seven ears of corn, and after burning them in the fire, with many foolish ceremonies, the whole company were allowed to feast upon *roasted corn*, and eat it in their cabins, after they went home. Before eating the green bean, they go over the same ceremony. When the corn gets hard, they have another frolic called the *green corn dance*, which lasts several days. In March, they used to have a yearly frolic called making *new fire*.[74]

George Foster, Sequoyah's early biographer, has succinctly characterized the green corn festival as known to his Oklahoma Cherokee informants in the 1880's:

The Green Corn Dance was the annual festival, the origin of which is not now known. At this the conjurer prepared a sort of medicine, on a day appointed by the old people, and seven families were appointed to furnish corn for the feast. Every one was obliged to take a portion of the medicine, and a portion was offered, by throwing corn into the fire before any one could eat. Before the feast it was unlawful to eat of the new corn of the season, and no person was ever known to transgress. After that all might eat freely.[75]

James Mooney was present at the last green corn festival to be held on the Qualla Reservation in 1887. He has left a brief notice of this ritual as well as of a surviving part of the rite which he observed in 1913 and 1914 and which is still observed by some families. Unfortunately, he published very little of his data on this ceremony, and his notes relating to this function have not been found among his papers in the archives of the Bureau of American Ethnology:

[74] Tuttle, 1833, pp. 147-48.   [75] Froste, 1885, pp. 57-58.

By special permission of some of the Indian priests Mr. Mooney was able to be present for the second time at the family ceremony of invoking the blessing upon the new corn and on those about to partake of it for the first time. This ceremony, probably never witnessed by another white man, is still strictly observed in private at their homes by most of the full-blood families before tasting the new corn of the season, the priests who conduct the rite going, while yet fasting, from house to house through the settlement for that purpose. The so-called Green Corn Dance, the great tribal celebration of thanksgiving for the new corn, was last performed in 1887, on which occasion Mr. Mooney was also present.[76]

Opportunity was also afforded for special studies and observations, particularly of the ceremonial "going to water," and augury with the beads to forecast the health prospect and lifespan of each member of the family, before partaking of the first corn of the new crop.[77]

Swimmer, one of Mooney's chief informants, wrote out the words of at least some of the songs and of one speech for the green corn festival in 1887. This manuscript is still preserved, but not transcribed and translated, in the archives of the Bureau of American Ethnology.[78] Part of the content of this ritual is doubtless missing. An attempt to interpret the manuscript with Cherokee informants failed, as these forms of the songs were unknown to them, and they felt that this lack of knowledge reflected on their dependability; however, the general contents of the manuscripts were outlined with the help of Will West Long, of the Big Cove. The sequence, is as follows:

I. An address of a chief to the people at a preliminary feast seven days before the green corn festival, setting the date and admonishing the people not to be drunk, to behave themselves, and not to interfere with others at the festival.

II. A series of sixteen songs called aniʻtɪkwɔlɛluhuskɑʼhi ("they have bulging foreheads").

[76] "Explorations," Smithsonian Institution, 1914, pp. 72–73.
[77] *Ibid.*, 1913, p. 64.   [78] Mooney, MS*b*.

III. A series of five wili'sa songs. This is the men's dance.
IV. A series of eight i·tsą ("meal") songs. This is the women's dance.
V. A series of ganaʔhiya'("along the trail") songs. According to Will West Long, guns are fired in this dance.
VI. A series of social and animal dances, as follows: friendship dance (ayɛ·lulehi' and dilsti"), buffalo dance, raccoon dance, pheasant dance, hog dance, corn dance, and running dance. Two bear dance songs and a medicine dance song are also included, but they doubtless pertain to other rituals, as may some of the other animal dances.

Will West Long, of Big Cove, dance leader and authority on Cherokee tradition, was familiar with the current green corn feast, and he functioned as a leader on occasions when its performance was required. He had not seen the periodic green corn festival. Drawing on information which he received from his mother, and from his older brother, however, he was able to supply some information about this extinct ceremony.

Will West Long's information revealed that this green corn festival was held the day and night before the first corn was to be eaten. A medicine was first prepared, and an emetic was drunk by everyone present, followed by "going to water."[79] Then the medicine was administered to all who were present at the ceremony. A formula may have accompanied the going to water,[80] but no formula was required as an accompaniment to the medicine that followed.[81] Then a series of animal and

[79] The "going to water" ordeal is an important item in Cherokee ritual. The purifying nature of the river was resorted to as a cleansing and protective symbol at almost any crisis in the life of the Cherokee individual or community. This formalized ceremonial bathing in the water of the river became an integral part of many ceremonial and curative procedures.

[80] Mooney and Olbrechts (1932, pp. 232–34) gave a formula like that used in this connection and (pp. 289–91) a formula used when "going to water" on the following morning.

[81] Cherokee medicinal practice and certain phases of Cherokee ritual depended in part on traditional spoken charms, called prayers and formulas by the Cherokee. These are memorized, must be spoken very exactly, and are the property of a semiprofessional "conjurer" class. These formulas have been

social dances lasted all night. This dance series seems to have been the same as that in the modern green corn feast used for curative purposes, described by Speck and discussed hereinafter.

In the morning the conjuror who served as dance leader took all the people "to water" again and then examined each person with the beads and cloth to see whether they would live until the next year's green corn festival. In this form of divination the conjuror places two beads (glass beads were used in recent time, but these were said to have replaced seeds of *Lithospermum*, uni·skǫ''—"heads"), one black and one red or white, on a piece of white cloth, the red (or white) bead to the conjuror's right. The cloth is provided by the person being examined and is given to the conjuror as a token payment. The conjuror then speaks to the beads after a fixed formula, asking first the red bead if the person is to live until the next year, and then asking the black bead the same question. If the red bead moves by itself, the person is expected to survive the year, and if the black bead moves, the patient will not live the year out.[82]

In case the divination indicated that someone would not live that long, a similar green corn feast was held at night. Dances

---

written in the syllabary invented by Sequoyah (also spelled Sequoya) about 1820, and some are no longer understandable because of the archaic forms preserved in them. It is probably the ritual language of these formulas to which Hicks refers as a forgotten language in the account previously quoted.

For a thorough study of Cherokee formulas and their function, see Mooney and Olbrechts, 1932.

[82] Divination seems to have been an important feature in Cherokee culture; it may even once have constituted a distinct profession. The observation of the motion of suspended magical stones and, more important, of beads laid on cloth or held between thumb and forefinger was resorted to in the foretelling of death, the diagnosis of disease, the finding of lost and stolen objects, and the discovery of the identity of a witch or conjuror responsible for magically caused disease, to mention but a few of the more important uses of these divination devices. Different formalized procedures were resorted to for different purposes, and in some cases even bits of roots or twigs were employed instead of beads.

were held and no person was allowed to sleep. The proper formulas were recited by the conjuror, and further divination by the beads was tried until it was found that the person would live. Then that person's life was believed to be secure until the next year.

Will West Long's brother, who died in 1904, was a leader at those ceremonies. According to Will, he once examined a girl with the beads under such circumstances, and he found that she would not live until the following summer. He attempted to arrange the feast which would prolong her life until the next year, but her family would not co-operate by providing a feast and helping with the ceremony. Therefore, it could not be held, and the girl died the following winter.

It is probably this secondary phase of the ceremony that has survived as a curative feature in association with certain forms of diagnoses and therapy. When one considers that among the central features of the green corn festivals of the Cherokee and Creek, as recorded by the earlier observers, the expiation of crime and the beginning anew of all phases of tribal life attracted much attention, the curative features of these ceremonies may also have been of great significance in aboriginal times.[83]

Some published notes of Mooney's contain traditions that relate to a period prior to the festival he observed:

> Just before the Green-corn dance, in the old times, every fire in the settlement was extinguished and all the people came and got new fire from the townhouse. This was called *atsi'la galûñkw?ti'yu*, "the honored or sacred fire."[84]
>
> Some say this everlasting fire was only in the larger mounds at Nikwasi, Kitu'hwa, and a few other towns, and that when the new fire was thus drawn up for the Green-corn dance, it was distributed from them to the other settlements.[85]
>
> From conversation with old Cherokee it seems probable that in cases where no satisfaction was made by the relatives of the man-

---

[83] Witthoft, 1946b, p. 215.
[84] Mooney, 1906, p. 396.   [85] *Ibid.*,

slayer, he continued to reside close within the limits of the town until the next recurrence of the annual Green-corn dance, when a general amnesty was proclaimed.[86] (Mooney here describes Chota as a peace and refuge town.)

At daybreak the whole party went down to the running stream, where the pupils or hearers of the myths stripped themselves, and were scratched upon their naked skin with a bone-tooth comb in the hands of the priest, after which they waded out, facing the rising sun, and dipped seven times under the water, while the priest recited prayers upon the bank. This purificatory rite, observed more than a century ago by Adair, is also a part of the ceremonial of the ballplay, the Green-corn dance, and in fact, every important ritual performance.[87]

Frank G. Speck, during the course of his extensive study of surviving Cherokee dances, observed and described a modern green corn ceremony still in existence in the Big Cove community of Qualla Reservation.[88] This ceremony, however, is not held at any fixed time and seems to have lost all connection with the cycle of the agricultural year. It is performed for curative purposes and for spiritual benefit at whatever time in the summer it may be needed by persons desiring spiritual help. The performance is accompanied by a feast provided by the patients or sponsors and their families. Apparently, one sequence of the old agricultural festival has continued its existence after the passing of the green corn festival, and has come into new associations, perhaps long before the major, fixed ceremony had been discontinued.

This ritual, as described by Speck from the account of several Big Cove informants, lasted a day and the following night. It is sponsored by some individual who feels a need for giving it in order to achieve some spiritual benefit and to avert or remedy poor health. Its additional functions are the prevention of illness resulting from eating green corn and the stimulation of the growth and bearing of the corn crop; it is allegorical of the men's and women's roles in Cherokee culture. The

---

[86] *Ibid.*, p. 207. [87] *Ibid.*, p. 230.
[88] Speck, MS*a*.

benefits of the ritual accrue to all who participate, but especially to the sponsors, and everyone around is invited to the ritual and to the feast accompanying it. There are no restrictions as to the foods which may be eaten during the ceremony.

The ceremony, consisting of both men's and women's parts which occur simultaneously and blend in certain parts of the procedure, is divided into four portions or stages. The first part, with some variations, consists of the men's dance (uli'ˈsį), which is held at a distance from the main dancing ground, and guns are fired. The women's dance (ˈᵋ·.łsɑ, "meal") is meantime held in the center of the main dance ground, with several different dance movements. Leg rattles are worn by the leader. The men sing responses to some of the women's songs. These two sets of dances continue simultaneously until afternoon, when the men's dance line surrounds the women's line and merges with it. The second stage is a feast provided by the women of the sponsoring group.

The third portion of the ritual occurs just before sundown. Men and women first dance separately, then, still carrying guns, the men surround the women's group and mingle with them, dancing to gourd rattles and the leg rattles of the woman leader, who is now in charge, until the sun has set (gɑnɑ'ni'·, "along the trail," is the name of the mixed stage of the dance).

The entire night is then spent in social and animal dances, starting with the friendship dance (in which men and women alternate), and concluding with the round dance (running dance), which, however, is preceded by the corn dance (selù ulskʻitɑ', "corn dance"). The other dances which might be performed were beaver dance, buffalo dance, pigeon dance, chicken dance, partridge ("pheasant") dance, ground hog dance, horse dance, knee-deep (small frog) dance, ant dance, raccoon dance, and gizzard (bird) dance. These animal dances are all somehow concerned with the placation of animal spirits and are said to have been learned from the mythical Stonecoat monster and culture-hero (a possible parallel to the Iroquois tradition of the origin of social dances from the Creator's evil-minded twin brother, "Flint"). Stonecoats are also prominent in the Iroquois literature.

Speck's informants called the green corn dance (the surviving green corn ceremony?) akɔhadį (literally "big foreheads in motion") and reported a tradition that the ceremony was named after a group of Cherokee called di·ni·kɔhįnǫ"("big foreheads projecting out"), who were most devout in performing this ceremony and who practiced head deformation, hence their name.[89] Mooney, in a manuscript of the 1880's, called the green corn dance a′năgahŭskŭ′·i.[90] If Will West Long's translations of the names of the dance songs of the 1887 manuscript are correct, a specific set of dance songs for the green corn festival bore a similar name. It was previously noted that a Seneca social dance, the bean or linking-arms dance, which is traditionally the evil twin brother's version of the Creator's traditional women's dance (tǫwi′·sas), specifically dedicated to corn, beans, and squash, tells of a young man's infatuation with an older woman who has bumps on her forehead. Other curious parallels, occurring in equivalent ceremonies in both groups, are extremely puzzling. More recent field studies of Allegany Seneca ceremonies by Merle H. Deardorff, of Warren, Pennsylvania, indicate that this dance (wen ontǫwisas) and its equivalent ritual performance are considered non-Iroquois in origin by Seneca informants and may represent the vestiges of an introduced ritual which has been added to the end of the Seneca green corn festival. The movements and the interplay of men's and women's parts, as described to me by Deardorff, suggest that the green corn ceremonies of the Southeast may show close relationship to this Iroquois ritual, which the Allegany Seneca consider a distinct rite. It is possible that this particular sequence was introduced among the Iroquois by adopted captives from the Cherokee country in the seventeenth or eighteenth century.[91]

[89] *Ibid.*
[90] Mooney, MS*b*.
[91] I am indebted to Mr. Deardorff for the use of his notes and for many helpful suggestions concerning various phases of Iroquois ethnology.

Jeremiah Curtin's Seneca origin story for the tǫnwi′sas rite tells of its introduction by two women who had been captured by the Cherokee and later escaped. They received supernatural aid during their escape and return home and received the songs in a vision while fleeing from the Cherokee.[92]

The only early account of Cherokee ceremonialism, made by John Howard Payne and David Buttrick about 1835, is preserved in the Newberry Library, Chicago,[93] but I have not yet had access to this material and must depend upon the published fragments until such time as I may be in Chicago. Unfortunately, these published fragments show very little correlation with the other Cherokee data, and in some ways suggest a Creek ceremonial cycle. Buttrick was for many years a missionary in the town of Chickamauga, which was a mixed community of Cherokee, Creek, Shawnee, and other peoples. It is possible that here the Cherokee, already losing the knowledge of their own ceremonial complex, adopted many Creek traits from their neighbors, or even that the ceremonies Buttrick described had taken on an international character.

E. G. Squier had access to these manuscripts about 1860, and reprinted parts in his appendix to Bartram's observations. More recently, W. H. Gilbert utilized the original manuscripts while engaged in field work among the Qualla Cherokee and published paraphrased parts of these manuscripts with some additional field notes. The parallel published extracts from the Payne manuscript follow:

2d Sah-looh stuknee, keel-steh-steeh; a preliminary or new green-corn feast, held when the young corn first became fit to taste.

3d Tung-noh-kaw-hoough-ni; mature or ripe green-corn festival, which succeeded the other in some 40 or 50 days, when the corn had become hard and perfect.[94]

2. The preliminary Green Corn Feast.—This is entitled sah-lookstiknee keehstehsteeh in the Payne Manuscripts and rendered selu

---

[92] Mooney, 1900, pp. 365-67.
[93] Payne, MS*b*.
[94] Bartram, 1853, p. 74 (footnote by E. G. Squier).

tsunistigistiyi, or "roasting ears" time, by present day informants. It was held in August when the young corn first became fit to taste.

3. The Green Corn Feast.—This is called tungnahkawhooghni in the Payne Manuscripts and is rendered donagohuni by present day informants. The ripe or mature Green Corn Feast succeeded the Preliminary Green Corn Feast of August in about 40 or 50 days in the middle or latter September when the corn had become hard or perfect and is still held.[95]

The name of the preliminary feast, as used by Payne and Gilbert, may possibly refer to the green corn medicine ritual which I have described and which Mooney witnessed in 1913 and 1914. (This ritual will be discussed hereinafter.) Gilbert's name for the main feast would appear to be di·ni·kɔhɛnɑ̨'' ("big foreheads projecting out"), the modern corn ceremony which Speck has described and which I have previously discussed.

Squier also reprinted a part of the Payne material describing the preliminary feast; this is included in Gilbert's reproduction of Payne's account, which is here presented:

The second great festival, the Preliminary New Green Corn Feast, was held in midsummer and at the time of the simultaneous ripening of the corn, or maize, throughout the nation. When the corn was found ripe, a messenger was despatched to gather seven ears, bring them back to the counselors, and assemble the people. A 6-day hunt was decreed for the hunters and the seven prime counselors fasted for 6 days at the national heptagon. When the hunters had shot the first buck, they cut a small piece from the right side of the end of the tongue. On the evening of the sixth day, the populace assembled at the national heptagon bringing in fresh ears of corn while the hunters brought in fresh meat. This night was spent in an all-night vigil and religious dance. On the seventh day, the festival began with the delivery of the seven ears of corn to the uku. New fire was made by a fire-maker on the alter from bark of seven selected trees. Leaves of old tobacco were sprinkled on the fire and omens were taken from this. The uku placed the seven ears in the fire also with the piece of deer's tongue and then prayed that the sacrifice might be acceptable. After this rite the uku and his seven counselors fasted for seven more days

[95] Gilbert, 1943, pp. 326-27.

and the populace then assembled for another general 1-day fast which completed the second festival.

The third great feast was the Mature, or Ripe Green Corn Feast, and was held in September 40 or 50 days after the preceding festival. First, the seven counselors summoned the honorable women for a religious dance and then fixed the festival for some time later. The usual pattern of behavior occurred, the hunters being sent out and special officers appointed to order the festival. An arbor of green boughs was framed in the sacred square of the national heptagon wherein a beautiful shade tree was located. A large booth was erected and seats laid out. On the evening prior to the festival day, the hunters and the people assembled and everyone took a green bough for the rites of the next day. All then retired early. On the ensuing noon the people paraded with green boughs held overhead. The uku who presided at this rite was given the special ceremonial title of Netagunghstah and was elevated on a platform held up by carriers and was dressed in a white robe with leggings, moccasins, otter skins on the legs, and a red cap on the head. Altogether this festival lasted 4 days and women were excluded from the sacred square during the dances. In the evenings they might mingle in the social dances, however. This festival was the most deeply rooted rite that the Cherokees had and lasted the longest. It is said to have been connected at one time with a festival of green boughs which was more distinctive and exclusive in its characteristics.[96]

The two Green Corn Feasts resemble each other and both were concerned with the ripening and harvesting of the corn and the rite of eating it. The details of these rites do not seem to have been well recorded but there was some fasting before the ceremonial partaking in the new corn.[97]

In the capital town of the tribe there was a national council consisting of the uku, his town attendants together with the white chiefs of the lower towns and their attendants. This national council was convened by the newly elected uku before a Green Corn Feast, and on emergency occasions, through the raising the uku's standard;. . .[98]

The two festivals described here may represent a preliminary feast given when the corn is first eaten, and a later one when the green corn is abundant. Hicks's brief sketch, previously

[96] *Ibid.*, pp. 329-30.
[97] *Ibid.*, p. 326.   [98] *Ibid.*, p. 323.

quoted, would suggest such a division, and there is some modern evidence of a similar first corn observance and later major celebration. Data derived from Will West Long, however, might indicate a recent splitting up of an older festival equivalent to the Creek ceremony, hereinafter discussed, into several parts in the process of disintegration of Cherokee culture, as I have suggested elsewhere:

... it appears that the Cherokee in aboriginal times celebrated a major community festival when the green corn first became mature enough to eat; this festival persisted, probably in an abbreviated form as late as 1887. Portions of this ritual became separated from the obsolescent Green Corn Festival and at present are found as two separate survivals, a Green Corn Feast held for curative purposes whenever it may be required and a Green Corn Medicine, which is prepared in the separate households of the more conservative Cherokee and administered to all members of the family as a prerequisite to eating the green corn. Continued adherence to this medicine ritual indicates the strong conservatism of a certain minority of "full-blood" Cherokee households.[99]

The green corn medicine, referred to above, possibly the survival of Payne's preliminary festival, is still observed by some of the Qualla Cherokee. The following account of this medicine is extracted, with some additions, from my previous article on this ritual.[100]

At present, in addition to the green corn feast, which is performed when required, the Cherokee has also preserved one other fragment of extreme importance. This is the green corn medicine, called both sɛ·lu' djwaʼnigę'·i da·nisdi' gisgą'nʻi ("corn soft, for they are eating") and se·lu'itsehiʻdanisdi' gi·sgą'nʻi ("corn, new or green, for they are eating"). Mooney's data on the 1913 observance, already quoted, would indicate that other features had survived as a part of the family ceremony until at least that date.

This green corn medicine, according to tradition, was a feature of the green corn festival and is probably represented in Hicks's account by the reference to "wild horehound." It is

[99] Witthoft, 1946b, p. 219.   [100] *Ibid.*

now no longer preceded by a purge, however, and is made and administered by the head of each household to his family; it is an individual, not a community function, and is performed whenever the family's green corn is ready to eat. According to Mollie Sequoyah, of the Big Cove, it is intended to prevent colic caused by eating corn, the primary food resource of the Cherokee, and one which is much relished. The people have been unaccustomed to eating green corn since the previous year, and its latency for harm or benefit is believed to be strong. Children especially require prophylactic treatment to avert sickness resulting from the first seasonal use of corn. Will West Long stated that it is intended to prevent the increase of stomach and intestinal worms, which otherwise would flourish on this choice food and do great damage to the person so rash as to eat of it without the medicinal preparative. None of the really conservative Indians of the Big Cove settlement would even taste green corn if they had not previously partaken of the medicine. I have seen Will look wistfully at "roasting ears" on the table of a neighbor with whom he was dining, but refuse the corn because his was not ready and he had not taken the medicine. Under similar circumstances, Mollie decided that she could eat the corn only because it was not a variety grown by the Indians, but "white man's corn," and so did not require this preventive measure.

The use of this medicine to inhibit the growth of parasitic worms from corn is not unparalleled, for Bartram noted a somewhat comparable prophylaxis for the same cause of illness among the Creeks:

> The hooping cough is fatal among their children, and worms very frequent. But (besides their well-known remedy, *spigelia anthelmentica*), to prevent the troublesome and fatal effects of this disease, they use a strong *lixivium* prepared from ashes of green stalks of beans and other vegetables, in all their food prepared from corn (*zea*), which otherwise, they say, breeds worms in their stomachs.[101]

[101] Bartram, 1853, p. 43. Swanton (1928a, pp. 553, 608) mentioned use of vermifuges at Creek green corn ceremonies.

The medicine itself is made up of the leaves of four or more different plants. Apparently, the recipe varies somewhat from family to family, but I do not have sufficient data to indicate how great the differences may be. These leaves are crushed in the hands, pounded together in the mortar used to crush corn into meal, and then steeped in warm water. The solution is drunk by all the members of the family. Then they are free to eat the unripe corn for the remainder of the season.

The plant ingredients used by Will West Long are listed in Table I. The use of the first three plants is obligatory, and any one of the remainder may be used as the fourth ingredient, the others being added if available. Will West Long explains that these plants are rampant cornfield weeds and are thus, he supposes, able to overcome the generative power of the corn imparted to the worms. The volunteer corn and the plant "resembling corn," are used because they appear to be dwarfed and weakly plants of the same sort as corn. Any other cornfield weed leaves may be added to the medicine if the preparator so desires. A vermifuge, such as *Artemesia*, might be as good, the informant suggests, but is not used in this association.

The medicine as prepared by Mollie Sequoyah consists of the leaves of four plants, used in exactly the same fashion. This medicine is required to prevent colic, which would plague anyone eating the new green corn without previously taking the medicine. It is especially necessary for children. The ingredients are as follows: galu⁺·na' ("gourd"), sɛ·lu'kwoyaʻ ("bearded wheat grass"), walelu'unig'egisti' ("jewelweed"), and u·wagaʻ ("volunteer corn").

There are several observances in force concerning the eating of the unripe corn. The corn is the gift of a culture heroine, whose name is sɛ·lu', the same name as that applied to corn, and the corn came from her body. These rules for treatment of the green corn and their explanation, as offered by Mollie Sequoyah, have their basis in the myth of the origin of corn, as do some of the features of the green corn festival.

One must not blow on a roasted ear of green corn in order to cool it, for this would cause a thunderstorm. The Thunders are the sons and husband of sɛ·lu', the Corn Mother, and would

TABLE I
Contents of the Cherokee Green Corn Medicine

Indian Name	Translation	English Name	Latin Name
sɛ·lu·kwo·ya'*	"Resembling corn"	Bearded wheat grass	*Apopyron caninum* (L.) R. & S.
toli'diy'usti'	"Sticks on you, like"	Adam's needle	*Yucca filamentosa* L.†
ɑwosɑ·ul'si'yenehi'	"Itself splitting or growing leaves"	Spiny amaranth	*Amaranthus spinosus* L.
unighis'o gohast'i'		Volunteer corn‡	*Zea mays* L.
walelu' unig'legisti'	"Humming bird, taking sap out of flower"	Wild lettuce	*Lactuca biflora* Walt.
galu'na'		Jewelweed	*Impatens biflora* Walt.§
wat'ska'		Gourd‖	*Cucurbita lagenaria* L.
ugwas'ta'luʸaddɑ'	"Sticking on"	Green amaranth	*Amaranthus retroflexus* L.
unistelęʸosti'¶	"Sticking out"	Ragweed	*Ambrosia trifida* L.
nistelę'·histi'	"Thistle like"	Wild comfrey	*Cynoglossum virginianum* L.
dᶻiᵈdᶻiyusti'		Ragweed	*Ambrosia elatior* L.
uniᵘdᶻiᵈdᶻiigoᵇᵘsdi'	"They are thistles scattering all over"		Not identified
			Not identified

* This name is used for both of the plants here listed, and either may be used in this medicine.

† According to Will West Long, the roots and leaves of the yucca are also soaked in warm water, and the potion drunk as a medicine for "sugar diabetes."

‡ This is merely corn that has seeded itself in a pasture or fallow field.

§ Leaves and flowers of this plant are also used, according to Mollie Sequoyah, as one ingredient in a tea that is given to a woman in childbirth to "make the child come quickly"; it is so used because of the explosive way in which the seeds fly out o their pods.

‖ According to Mollie Sequoyah, gourd seeds are mashed and soaked in hot water, and the potion is drunk to cure inability to urinate. This is probably related to the white peoples' use of pumpkin seed for the same purpose.

¶ This name is the general Cherokee term for bur-bearing plants, but the plant specimen was collected with the informant (as also in other cases). This plant is used as one ingredient in several compound medicines recorded by Mooney and Olbrechts, 1932, pp. 119, 174.

resent such disrespectful treatment of her. After the green corn has been eaten, the cobs must be kept in the house for four days, because sɛ·lu"'s body lay outdoors on the ground for that length of time after she had been killed by her son. The all-night dancing and wakefulness of the green corn festival are the observation of the original admonition that they should stay awake all night and dance, so that the corn would grow and mature overnight. Seneca informants also told me that corn and other crops grow at night.

According to Will West Long, a medicine of the steeped leaves of the hog peanut, *Apios tuberosa* L. (tuya'ⁱyusti', "like a bean"), was drunk in the usual manner before the first green beans were eaten, but this medicine was last used in the Big Cove about 1890. Hicks's account, previously quoted, mentions this medicine. The Creeks of Cowassawday also held some festival at this time.[102]

According to Moses Owl, and Jimsie and Takwat Wallace, of Birdtown (another community of Qualla Reservation), the green corn festival and the green corn medicine have not been used at Birdtown in the last century. The recipe for the medicine is lost, but it is said that it included cornstalks and the leaves of the barren strawberry, *Waldsteinia* (antǫⁱyusti', "like a strawberry"), and was drunk before the green corn festival.

Moses Owl offered some information that he had obtained from his grandmother, who had attended green corn festivals at Governor's Island, North Carolina, prior to the removal (1838). These ceremonies were held at or near the mound on the Ferguson Farm at Governor's Island and were attended not only by Cherokee but also by Creek and other Indians. One festival culminated in a vicious brawl between Creek and Cherokee participants. In this account earth was carried to the dance ground and spread on a rectangular area, and Moses supposed that the mound had been built up by such accumulations. He has heard that only persons who died during the green corn festival were buried in this mound.

The carrying in of fresh earth to cover the ceremonial ground

---

[102] Swanton, 1928a, p. 568.

is typical of the Creek ceremony, but is not noted for Cherokee. Bartram saw no such prepared squares in use in the Cherokee country, whereas they were abundant in the Creek territories.[103]

The Cherokee green corn festival, as known from recent accounts, has survived as two rituals. A preliminary ceremony concerned with the prevention of illness which may result from eating green corn, is followed by a major ceremony intended to propitiate the corn and to be allegorical of the functions of men and women in Cherokee cultural life. There is some evidence from modern ethnology that these two ceremonial procedures were originally parts of one festival, but their separate observances are noted in the earlier accounts. The modern preliminary ritual consists mainly of the administration of an herb medicine; in Payne's account both green corn ceremonies are very similar in content. The preliminary ceremony shows some resemblance to the busk (the green corn ceremony of the Creeks). Later phases of the busk resemble somewhat the Cherokee second green corn festival. The parallels will be indicated in the discussion of the Creek ritual.

Certain features of the Cherokee ceremonies may be noted as distinctive. The attention in the ritual to the number seven, symbolic of the seven Cherokee clans, is noteworthy in Payne's description. The townhouse was seven-sided, the preliminary festival lasted seven days, seven ears of corn were sacrificed, and the fast was of seven days' duration. The square ground is described,[104] and Gilbert's summary indicates that an arbor of green boughs was included in this square, and possibly a tree. The division between sacred and social dances is noted. In later accounts these features are not recorded, and very little correlation exists between Payne's account and the modern observations; Hicks's and Foster's accounts check better with modern data than does Payne's account. A seven-sided ceremonial ground has been noted for several Oklahoma Cherokee communities, but I have no information on the associated cere-

[103] Bartram, 1853, p. 36.
[104] Squier (1851, pp. 239-40) quoted Payne's description of the Cherokee townhouse and squareground.

monies.¹⁰⁵ More data from both historic and living sources of information would no doubt bridge the spaces between Payne's data and recent North Carolina Cherokee observations.

THE SOUTHEASTERN SIOUAN TRIBES

ALTHOUGH the southeastern Siouan-speaking peoples may quite possibly have stressed ceremonial observances concerned with various phases of an agricultural year-cycle, there is little evidence of the existence of maize ceremonies among these tribes, either from the sparse historical material or from the surviving Catawba. Lawson has left two references which merely suggest the possibility of a green corn ritual. In his journal under an entry made between September 15 and November 17, 1700, he mentioned a Waxsaw ceremony:

> It happened to be one of their great Feasts, when we were there: ... This feast was held in commemoration of the plentiful Harvest of Corn they had reaped the summer before, with an united Supplication for like plentiful Produce the Year ensuing.¹⁰⁶

This would appear to have been a harvest festival, but this is the only certain reference to any maize ceremonialism among these people. If a green corn ritual were also observed, no evidence of it now exists. Another note of Lawson's may refer to either some group of Siouan or Algonkian peoples of the Carolinas, or perhaps to the Tuscarora; it may represent a generalization derived from all of the tribes of this area. It possibly refers to a harvest festival:

> They have a third of Feasts and Dances, which are always when the Harvest of Corn is ended, and in the Spring. The one, to return Thanks to the good Spirit, for the Fruits of the Earth; the other, to beg the same Blessings for the succeeding Year.¹⁰⁷

The only data from the surviving remnants of the southeastern Siouans comes from the Tutelo descendants of Six Nation's Reserve, Ontario, Canada, where Speck recorded some

---

¹⁰⁵ Swanton, 1928a, p. 603.
¹⁰⁶ Lawson, 1714, p. 36.   ¹⁰⁷ *Ibid.*, p. 174.

ethnological data on Tutelo rituals and recorded songs associated with a harvest ritual.[108] Whether this observance represents a green corn or harvest festival, or both, is not certain. The ritual lasted for four nights and included the following dance songs:

Four nights songs. These have been adopted by the Cayuga, Onondaga, and Seneca longhouses as social dances and are known as the four nights songs.[109]

Bean dance. This has been adopted by the Sour Spring Cayuga, and seems to be the same dance as the bean dance or linking-arms dance among the Coldspring Seneca, discussed earlier.

Feather dance. This is apparently a Tutelo adoption of one of the four sacred ceremonies of the Iroquois, with Tutelo songs.

Adǫnwa'. This is another of the Iroquois sacred ceremonies, adopted by the Tutelo and fitted out with songs in the Tutelo language.

This ceremony, held in October when all the crops were harvested, lasted four nights, each night being spent at the house of a different family. The four nights songs constituted a thanksgiving for all the crops and were sung during most of each night, only the women dancing. The bean dance was for men and women, who danced in two rings, the women forming the outer circle. The participants represented the growing corn and beans. This pattern suggests the Iroquois women's rite discussed previously, but not enough data are available for adequate comparison.

This festival has some curious relationships to the Iroquois ceremonies. All of the dances noted in its content are performed by the Sour Spring Cayuga and doubtless by other Iroquois communities; two of these ceremonial features were borrowed from the Iroquois four sacred ceremonies. The other two ceremonies may be Tutelo in origin. It would appear that this ceremony has been vastly modified by Iroquois influence, and it would be unwise to draw any conclusions as to the original agricultural ceremonies of the Tutelo. Even more significant

[108] Speck, 1942, pp. 18–20.   [109] Fenton, MS*a*.

is the probability that this was a late harvest festival; the other Siouan reference would also indicate the emphasis on this time of the year for the ritual thanksgiving for the crops. It should also be noted that the content suggests the Iroquois harvest as much as the green corn festival for the Iroquois model. From the scant data available, the Iroquois harvest festivals would seem to be very similar in content to the green corn festivals.[110]

The data from the southeastern Siouan peoples are too inadequate to venture any conjecture as to the significance of their maize ceremonialism. The only modern data on such an observance reflect little except Iroquois ritual. Poverty of material does not indicate the insignificance of such ritual among these peoples, but it is possible that these Siouans were peripheral to more agricultural peoples in the Southeast and that their economy did not stress agriculture to the same extent.

THE CREEK INDIANS AND THEIR NEIGHBORS

THE green corn festival as observed in the towns of the Creek Nation and their neighbors of the Southeast is generally called the busk (Creek *posketa*, a "fast").[111] It has probably attracted more attention than any other ceremony in the East. Several good descriptions were written by persons who witnessed these extended rituals, yet no complete study of the busk of any single town of the Creek Nation exists. No ethnologist has attempted to interpret any large part of the phenomena observed in one of these ceremonies through the medium of texts or through interpretations and explanations given by native informants. This situation reflects greater emphasis by students of Southeastern ethnohistory on historical documents than on ethnographic studies. As a result one may expect to find some confusion in the data on agricultural ceremonies in this area, and one can only interpret the green corn festival by piecing together fragments of information from various localities and times. This is especially dangerous, because recent data from the Oklahoma Creeks and

[110] Morgan, 1851, pp. 206-7.
[111] Loughridge and Hodge, 1890, pp. 28, 175.

from the Florida Seminole indicate that considerable modification may have taken place in the content and function of these festivals. Nevertheless, sufficient material exists to give at least as good a picture of Creek green corn ceremonialism as could be drawn for any other ethnic group.

Earlier students of the American Indian took great interest in the busk because it was the most conspicuous ceremony in this area and because the content, functions, and time of occurrence of this festival suggested that it was a broken-down survival of the Hebrew Passover. Thus, they recorded many more specific details of the ritual than most observers of this period were inclined to do. John Adair, a trader for some years among the Creek, Cherokee, and Chickasaw towns, in his ambitious attempt to demonstrate the origin and ethnic relationships of the American Indian, recorded much specific data, selected, however, by his emphasis on Hebrew and Tartar parallels. He has left the first significant account of the busk, although it is not known whether he described the busk as performed at Coosa, or whether, more likely, his account is a synthetic description made up of various observations from different towns and tribes of the Creek-Cherokee-Chickasaw region. His notes are spread over twenty-five pages of his book, interspersed with other data and with many fanciful interpretations. This busk would appear to have been a four-day festival, but the account is confused.

Adair's account of the preliminary procedure mentions the painting of the "war-cabin" with red clay, or blood-root, and the "white temple" with white clay (two of the sheds at the sides of the square), the cleansing of these structures, and the placing of new cane mats on the seats. The hearth was rebuilt; roots of button snakeroot, leaves of Indian tobacco, and ears of corn were enclosed in it. Presumably, the square ground was prepared at this time.[112]

After these preparations had been made, the materials for making the new fire were gathered, and a three-day fast began. Dry scratching was administered as a punishment (for having eaten green corn or breaking other taboos?). The "drivers"

[112] Adair, 1930, pp. 103-7.

(policemen) were placed in their positions on the square ground, and the participants partook of a purge made of the button snakeroot and chewed and ate the Indian tobacco. This purging continued for three days, while the priest secluded himself in a separate hut.[113]

Apparently, on the third day the fast was broken with a meal of last year's food (corn bread, etc.). The people retired, and the new fire was made with a fire drill, caught in shavings, fanned to flame with a swan's wing, and carried to the hearth in an old pottery vessel. This fire is called esakaáta emishe, "breath master"[114] (a term in the Chickasaw language?).

When the new fire has been started, the first fruits (green corn?), bear oil, meat, button snakeroot, and *Ilex cassena* were sacrificed to the fire. Offerings of the drinks were poured over the red and white seats.[115] Omens were drawn from the burning of the meat.[116]

The cassena was parched brown on the "altar," boiled, and served in consecrated conch shell vessels; "of this they drink now and then, till the end of the festival, and on every other religious occasion from year to year." Some old men purged themselves very severely by drinking to excess. Salt was tabooed until the fourth day of the festival.[117]

The altar, or hearth, to which the new fire was carried, at which the sacrifices were made, and where the black drink was prepared, may have been the hearth in the square ground.[118]

Adair's brief description of the conclusion, probably the fourth day of the festival, mentions a men's dance with pot drum and gourd rattles in which the participants were dressed in martial array; they carried white feathers or feather wands, and danced in three circles. Then these men repainted, dressed, and held a mock battle, which was followed by a grand mixed dance of three circles. The participants then painted themselves white and "went to water" (the ceremonial equivalent of the Cherokee water-ordeal ritual previously described).[119]

[113] *Ibid.*, pp. 107–9.
[114] *Ibid.*, pp. 110–11.　[115] *Ibid.*, p. 121.　[116] *Ibid.*, pp. 114–15.
[117] *Ibid.*, pp. 116–17.　[118] *Ibid.*, pp. 101–2.　[119] *Ibid.*, pp. 103–4.

GREEN CORN CEREMONIALISM

In another section Adair gives a more complete description of the last dance ritual of this sequence:

> While their sanctified new fruits are dressing, a religious attendant is ordered to call six of their old beloved women to come to the temple, and dance the beloved dance with joyful hearts, according to the old beloved speech. They cheerfully obey, and enter the supposed holy ground in solemn procession, each carrying in her hand a bundle of small branches of various green trees; and they join the same number of old magi, or priests, who carry a cane in one hand adorned with white feathers, having likewise green boughs in their other hand, which they pulled from their holy arbor, and carefully place there, encircling it with several rounds.
>
> The beloved men have their heads dressed with white plumes; but the women are decked in their finest, and annointed with bears grease having small tortoise-shells, and white pebbles, fastened to a piece of white-drest deer-skin, which is tied to each of their legs.
>
> At the end of this notable religious dance, the old beloved, or holy women return home to hasten the feast of the new sanctified fruits. In the meanwhile, everyone at the temple drinks very plentifully of the Cassena and other bitter liquids, to cleanse their sinful bodies; after which, they go to some convenient deep water, and there, according to the ceremonial law of the Hebrews, they wash away their sins with water. Thus sanctified, they return with joyful hearts in solemn procession, till they enter into the holy ground to eat of the new delicious fruits of wild canaan, etc.[120]

In the speeches preliminary to the dancing and feasting of the last day, the priest charges the people not to eat any "unsanctified, or impure food, otherwise they will get full of worms, and be devoured by famine and diseases,"[121] thus rationalizing the green corn ritual in the same terms as do the modern Cherokee.

John R. Swanton has fitted all of Adair's scraps together into a continuous narrative, which is easier to follow than the original.[122]

Adair, however, does not indicate the exact sequence of the features of this festival and has omitted any mention of certain

---

[120] *Ibid.*, p. 116.
[121] *Ibid.*   [122] Swanton, 1928a, pp. 590–601.

parts of the ceremony. His description is not so much an outline as a compilation of fragments that one would like to fit into a demonstrable sequence. Other accounts may supply this outline, but different procedures were no doubt followed in different towns, and Adair's account cannot be interpreted strictly in the light of other data.

The most revealing sketch of the busk as performed in the eighteenth century in the Creek town of Little Talasi (Otciapofa) was written by Alexander M'Gillivray, noted chief of the Creek nation, and was included in Charles Swan's *Position and State of Manners and Arts in the Creek, or Muskogee Nation in 1791*.[123] This author did not give a miscellany of observations, but he was sure of his data and gave a brief outline, including the features that were to him the most significant. This is the only early account of the busk written by a Creek, and is the most dependable early source:

The ceremony of the busk is the most important and serious of any observed by the Creek Indians.

It is the offering up of their first fruits, or an annual sacrifice, always celebrated about harvest time.

When corn is ripe, and the cassina or new black-drink has come to perfection, the busking begins on the morning of a day appointed by the priest, or *fire-maker* (as he is styled) of the town, and is celebrated for four days successively.

On the morning of the first day, the priest, dressed in white leather moccasins and stockings, with a white dressed deer-skin over his shoulders, repairs at break of day, unattended, to the square. His first business is to create the new fire which he accomplishes by much labor by the friction of two dry sticks. After the fire is produced, four young men enter at the openings of the four corners of the square, each having a stick of wood for the new fire; they approach the new fire with much reverence, and place the ends of the wood they carry, in a very formal manner, to it. After the fire is sufficiently kindled, four other young men come forward in the same manner, each having a fair ear of new corn, which the priest takes from them, and places with great solemnity in the fire, where it is consumed. Four young warriors then enter the square in the manner before mentioned, each

[123] Schoolcraft, 1860, 5: 251–83.

having some of the new cassina. A small part of it is given to the new fire by the priest, and the remainder is immediately parched and cooked for use. During these formalities, the priest is continually muttering some mysterious jargon which nobody understands, nor is it proper for any inquiries to be made on the subject; the people in general believe that he is then communicating with the *great master of breath*.

At this time, the warriors and others being assembled, they proceed to drink black drink in their usual manner. Some of the new fire is next carried and left on the outside of the square, for public use; and the women were allowed to come and take it to their several houses, which have the day before been cleaned and decorated with green boughs, for its reception; all the old fire in the town having been previously extinguished, and the ashes swept clean away, to make room for the new. During this day, the women are suffered to dance with the children on the outside of the square, but by no means suffered to come into it. The men keep entirely by themselves, and sleep in the square.

The second day is devoted by the men to taking their war-physic. It is a strong decoction of the button snake-root, or senneca, which they use in such quantities as often to injure their health, by producing spasms, etc.

The third day is spent by the young men in hunting or fishing, while the elder ones remain in the square and sleep, or continue their black drink, war-physic, etc., as they choose. During the first three days of busking, while the men are physicking, the women are constantly bathing. It is unlawful for any man to touch one of them, even with the tip of his finger; and both sexes abstain rigidly from all kinds of food or sustenance, and more particularly from salt.

On the fourth day, the whole town are assembled in the square, men, women and children promiscuously, and devoted to conviviality. All the game killed the day before by the young hunters, is given to the public; large quantities of new corn, and other provisions, are collected and cooked by the women over the new fire. The whole body of the square is occupied with pots and pans of cooked provisions, and they all partake in general festivity. The evening is spent in dancing, or other trifling amusements, and the ceremony is concluded.

N.B. All the provisions that remain are a perquisite to the old priest, or fire-maker.

ANTHONY. ALEX. M'GILLIVRAY[124]

[124] *Ibid.*, pp. 267–68.

Le Clerc Milfort, a French adventurer, spent about twenty years in the Creek Country as a friend and follower of Alexander M'Gillivray during his rise to power; he married M'Gillivray's sister. His memoir, a book of slightly dubious value, contains a notable account of the Creek busk, probably that of Otciapofa:

> Ils n'ont pas une religion déterminéd; quoi-qu'ils reconnoissent le grand maitre du souffle, ils n'ont aucunes cérémonies religieuses. Chaque année, au mois d'aout, ils s'assemblent par habitation pour célébrer la fete des moisons; alors its renouvellent tout ce qui leur a servi dans le courant de l'année qui vient d'expirer; les femmes cassent et brisent tout ce qui compose leur ménage, et le remontent à neuf. C'est ce meme jour que l'on mange, pour la première fois, du bled nouveau, et que le pretre ou medécine du canton allume un feu nouveau, et distribue à tous les hommes assistans la nouvelle medécine de guerre. Les Sauvages sont si religieus observateurs de cette cérémonie, que celui d'entr'eus qui n'auroit pas de maïs ancien pour se nourrir jusju'a cette epogue, mangeroit de racines plutot que de toucher au nouveau maïs. C'est également l'epoque ou l'on oublie et pardonne tous les motif des querells. Un Sauvage qui, après la fête, rappeleroit une ancienne querelle, seroit blamé par tous les autres.[125]

William Bartram's notes on the busk are apparently at second hand and are mainly concerned with the new fire rite:

> They venerate *Fire*, and have some mysterious rites and ceremonies which I could never perfectly comprehend.
> They seem to keep the *Eternal Fire* in the Great Rotunda, where it is guarded by the priests.
> In their great annual festival, called the *Busque* or feast of *First Fruits*, they put out all the fires of the nation or town; and then the high priest, by friction of dry woods, and the addition of *resin*, produces new fire in the Great Temple or Rotunda, from whence the whole town is supplied. But so far are the Muscogulges from having a corps of consecrated virgins to guard and keep this fire, that the women are not allowed to step within the pale of the Rotunda, and it is death for any to enter it. None but a priest can carry the fire forth.[126]

---

[125] Milfort, 1802, pp. 216–17.   [126] Bartram, 1853, pp. 26–27.

Bartram's description of the busk of one of the upper Creek towns, perhaps Atasi, varies considerably from other accounts.[127] The fasting and medication lasted three days, the new fire and the feast of new corn were prepared on the fourth day, and the feasting and dancing continued for three days, followed by four days of entertainment of friends from neighboring towns. They collected all their old clothing, pots, furniture, grain, and all old things while cleaning their households, and burned them in a common heap, a radical finish to the old year.

Another description of a Creek busk is a well-known outline by Benjamin Hawkins, an Indian agent in the last part of the eighteenth century. He described the eight-day busk of Kasihta, as observed, apparently, in the 1790's; his account is the only full outline of the eight-day ceremony:

Boos-ke-tau

This annual festival is celebrated in the months of July or August. The precise time is fixed by the Mic-co and counsellors, and is sooner or later, as the state of the affairs of the town, or the early or lateness of their corn, will suit for it. In Cussetuh, this ceremony lasts for eight days. In some towns of less note, it is but four days.

First Day

In the morning, the warriors clean the yeard of the square, and sprinkle white sand, when the a-cee (decoction of the cassine yupon) is made. The fire-maker makes the fire as early in the morning as he can, by friction. The warriors cut and bring into the square, four logs, as long each as a man can cover by extending two arms; these are placed in the centre of the square end to end, forming a cross, the outer ends pointed to the cardinal points; in the centre of the cross, the new fire is made. During the first four days, they burn out these four logs.

The pin-e-bun-gau (turkey dance) is danced by the women of the turkey tribe; and while they are dancing the possau is brewed. This is a powerful emetic. The possau is drank from twelve o'clock to the middle of the afternoon. After this, the Toc-oo-yule-gau (tadpole) is danced by four men and four women. (In the evening, the men

---

[127] Bartram, 1791, p. 508.

dance E-ne-hou-bun-gau, the dance of the people second in command.) This they dance till daylight.

Second Day

This day, about ten o'clock, the women dance Its-ho-bun-gau, (gun dance). After twelve, the men go to the new fire, take some of the ashes, rub them on the chin, neck and belly, and jump head foremost into the river, and they return into the square. The women having prepared the new corn for the feast, the men take some of it and rub it between their hands, then on their face and breasts, and then they feast.

Third Day

The men sit in the square.

Fourth Day

The women go early in the morning and get the new fire, clean out their hearths, sprinkle them with sand, and make their fires. The men finish burning out the first four logs, and they take ashes, rub them on their chin, neck and belly, and they go into the water. This day they eat malt, and they dance Obungauchapco (the long dance).

Fifth Day

They get four new logs, and place them as on the first day, and they drink a-cee, a strong decoction of the cassine yupon.

Sixth Day

They remain in the square.

Seventh Day

Is spent in like manner as the sixth.

Eighth Day

They get two large pots, and their physic plants, 1st. Mic-co-ho-yon-e-juh. 2. Toloh. 3. A-che-nau. 4. Cup-pau-pos-cau. 5. Chu-lis-sau, the roots. 6. Tuck-thlau-lus-te. 7. Tote-cul-hil-lis-so-wau. 8. Cho-feinsuck-cau-fuck-au. 9. Cho-fe-mus-see. 10. Hil-lis-hut-ke. 11. To-te-cuh chooo-his-see. 12. Welau-nuh. 13. Oak-chon-utch-oo. 14. Co-hal-le-wau-gee. These are all put into the pots and beat up with water.

The chemists (E-lic-chul-gee, called by the traders physic makers) they blow in it through a small reed, and then it is drank by the men, and rubbed over their joints till the afternoon.

They collect old corn cobs and pine burs, put them into a pot, and burn them to ashes. Four virgins who have never had their menses, bring ashes from their houses, put them in the pot and stir all together. The men take white clay and mix it with water in two pans. One pan of the clay and one of the ashes, are carried to the cabin of the Mic-co, and the other two to that of the warriors. They then rub themselves with the clay and ashes. Two men appointed to that office, bring some flowers of tobacco of a small kind (Itch-au-chu-le-puc-pug-gee) of, as the name imports, the old man's tobacco, which was prepared on the first day, and put in a pan on the cabin of the Mic-co, and they give a little of it to every one present.

The Mic-co and counsellors then go four times round the fire, and every time they face the east, they throw some of the flowers into the fire. They then go and stand to the west. The warriors then repeat the same ceremony.

A cane is stuck up at the cabin of the Mic-co with two white feathers in the end of it. One of the Fish tribe (Thlot-lo-ul-gee) takes it just as the sun goes down, and goes off towards the river, all following him. When he gets half way to the river, he gives the death whoop; this whoop he repeats four times, between the square and the water's edge. Here they all place themselves as thick as they can stand, near the edge of the water. He sticks up the cane at the water's edge, and they all put a grain of the old man's tobacco on their heads and in each ear. Then, at a signal given, four different times, they throw some into the river, and every man at the like signal plunges into the river, and picks up four stones from the bottom. With these they cross themselves on their breasts four times, each time throwing a stone into the river, and giving the death whoop; they then wash themselves, take up the cane and feathers, return and stick it up in the square, and visit through the town. At night they dance O-bun-gau Haujo (mad dance), and this finishes the ceremony.

This happy institution of the Boos-ke-tuh, restores man to himself, to his family and to his nation. It is a general amnesty, which not only absolves the Indians from all crimes, murder only excepted, but seems to bury guilt itself in oblivion.[128]

[128] Hawkins, 1848, pp. 75–77.

Adam Hodgson, about 1820, jotted down some information he had from a trader, apparently referring to the busk at Kasihta:

Before the corn turns yellow, the inhabitants of each town or district assemble; and a certain number enter the streets of what is more properly called the town, with the war-whoop and savage yells, firing their guns into the air, and going several times around the pole. They then take emetics, and fast two days; dancing around the pole a great part of the night. All the fires in the township are then extinguished, and the hearths cleared, and new fires kindled by rubbing two sticks. After this, they parch some of the new corn, and, feasting a little, disperse to their several homes. Many of the old chiefs are of opinion, that their ancestors intended this ceremony as a thank offering to the Supreme Being, for the fruits of the earth, and for success in hunting or war.[129]

Here is a Creek reference to what appears to be a centerpole. The date is noted, and a good observation of the function of the ceremony occurs. This busk appears to have been a four-day ceremony, and the sequence does not agree with that of Hawkins; the observations were probably from some other settlement than Kasihta.

My last description of a busk held east of the Mississippi is also the most thorough and best report on Creek ceremonialism. In 1835–36 John Howard Payne traveled in the Creek and Cherokee country; he had an intense interest in Indian customs, and he carried a small ledger into which he had copied a manuscript, William Bartram's letter to Benjamin S. Barton, later published as *Observations on the Creek and Cherokee Indians*. He attended the busk at the Creek town of Tukabatchie and kept a diary containing an account of the proceedings; this amounted to some twenty pages in the center of the notebook. He also incorporated some very interesting data and interpretations derived from Indian informants. This was Payne's first excursion into the Indian country, earlier than his Cherokee studies discussed above, and his enthusiasms and his artist's

---

[129] Hodgson, 1823, p. 268.

attention to detail are admirably displayed. Later, this account was incorporated into a letter to a relative in New York, cut out of the notebook, and sent by means of another traveler. A one-page postscript, dated August 12, 1835, in which Payne noted that he has substantiated all of his observations by careful questioning of Indians, was not separated from the notebook. The letter which had been removed was published in 1862.[130] The remaining manuscript was among Payne's effects when he died in Tunis and is now preserved in the Pennsylvania Historical Society Library, Philadelphia.[131] This may be the source of Squier's published version, although differences are evident. Swanton discovered the published account too late for inclusion in his major works and republished it separately, with a brief introduction and a few notes.[132] The neglect of Payne's study is unfortunate, for he clearly described distinctive features which have been overlooked in other sources and by later students of the Southeast. Other Creek data gathered by Payne exist in the Ayer Collection in Chicago[133] and may include material of primary significance, but I do not yet have access to this source. Payne apparently gathered data and recorded observations after a fashion typical of good modern ethnography. It is unfortunate that his literary remains were distributed at his death and have not been accessible to later students.

The account as written by Payne is an indispensable document to any student of the Southeast, but is far too long to reproduce here. A résumé of the description, however, seems worthwhile.

The Creek year began with the green corn festival (Payne seems to have been the first to use this term), and it was considered infamous to taste the corn before this ceremony. Chiefs of all the towns forming any particular clan met prior to the green corn season, to give orders for the manufacture of pottery vessels for the medicines. A second meeting was held to order new mats for the seats of the assembly. At a third meeting the date was apparently set, and bundles of sticks for a day-count

[130] Payne, 1862. [131] Payne, MS*a*.
[132] Swanton, 1922. [133] Payne, MS*b*.

were distributed to representatives of the families involved, who removed one stick each day until the set date, when everyone appeared at the square ground.

An ample square with four log sheds, one at each side, was formed far from any habitation. These four shelters, which were built of logs and wattle and were open only on the inside toward the square, were built up chin-high on the outside, and roofed; they contained broad benches or "beds," covered with matting. A thick, notched "mast" was attached to the inner side of each house, and during the festival each "mast" supported a bundle of tall canes hung with black and white feathers. The posts and roof beams of the four houses were decorated with "rude paint-daubs." At each angle was a broad open space between the house structures. Outside of one of these corners was the "council house" (townhouse), a high, conical, circular building with a low door apparently below ground level. Next to this was another square, sided by cornfields, backed by an earth ridge, and fronting on one of the house structures. In the center was a high circular mound, composed of sweepings and scraped-off earth from the annual preparation of the square ground. Each year the old surface of the square ground was removed and fresh earth strewn over it, after which all strangers and persons who had not observed the dietary and other taboos were excluded from this sanctified area. Just outside one corner of the second square was another small mound made up of the accumulated ashes of the busk fires, which were required to be gathered and carefully preserved. Women, strangers, persons who broke their fast or tasted liquor, and anyone touching a white man were excluded from the square ground.

Before the festival began and prior to the preparation of the square ground, a women's dance was held in the square, after which the women separated from the men until the conclusion of the fast. After the square was prepared, all of the fires in the district were extinguished, and all dwellings swept and washed. This ritual end of the old year was marked by the cessation of all enmities and the pardon of all sentenced criminals who could slip into the gathering at the beginning of the ceremonies. The fire was started by fire chiefs, with a square board, tinder, and a stock twirled in a hollow in the board. The original flame was carried to the center of the square, where a fire was lighted and the medicines were prepared in the new pottery vessels; brands were carried to all the households of the community. Drinking gourds were set on a bench, and officers guarded and prepared the black drink with great formality and ceremony.

The people were seated in the buildings; the chiefs stood at the edges of the square. The long-drawn-out, single-note refrains noted by Adair and others as specific to the black drink ceremony were repeated thrice, and the chiefs formed two diagonal lines across the square, with their backs to opposite corners. In succession they each took a draught of the black drink and after a few seconds ejected what they had swallowed, without moving a muscle; then two attendants passed gourds of the liquor to other persons, who remained in their places. A chief made a speech from his place, charging the participants to continue faithful to their traditional rituals and explaining some of the ritualistic features which were to follow.

Another chief walked around giving directions; gourd rattles, painted white, were produced by men who took stations on mats. All of the men participated in a dance in which feather fans were carried, and each person raised his hands over the fire at a special point in the dance circuit (feather dance of recent accounts?). The pace of the dance increased until all uttered a loud whoop, stopped, and then, running from the square, went to the river and performed the "going to water" ritual. They returned to the square and performed other dances; one dance pertained to the ball game and some appear to have been animal dances.

Here Payne, noting the inability of the interpreters to understand the content of some of the speeches and dance songs, made an observation reminiscent of Hicks's and M'Gillivray's comments about the use of an esoteric language on these occasions, and, incidently, touched upon the slight knowledge of their kinsfolk displayed even by the professional interpreters:

> But even their language, on these occasions, seems, by their own admission, beyond the learning of the "linkisters" (linguists). It is

a poetical, mystical idiom, varying essentially from that of trading and of familiar intercommunication, and utterly incomprehensible to the literal minds of mere trafficking explainers. Even were it otherwise, the persons hovering upon the frontiers most ingenuously own, when pressed for interpretations of Indian customs, that they care nothing for the Indians excepting to get their lands, and that they really consider all study concerning them as egregious folly, save only that of finding out how much cotton their grounds must yield and in what way the greatest speculations can be accomplished with the smallest capital.[134]

The last ceremony consisted of a scratching ordeal for boys and young men; this rite was held at the backs of the four buildings and at the back of the council house. The scratching was restricted to the legs; the blood was scooped off by those submitting to the ordeal and dashed against the outside of the back walls of these buildings.

A shed of loose boards on posts, covering a raised platform, was provided in a field near by, and Payne slept here in preference to staying in the adjacent white town of Tallasse. The dancing (apparently social dances), and stirring of the medicine (with sung incantations) continued all night.

On the morning of the second day the whole black drink ceremony was repeated, and two ancient circular shields of copper and steel were now borne in the dance, sacred paraphernalia produced only on great occasions. Ears of green corn had previously been brought in and presented to a chief, who repeated an invocation that the corn might continue plentiful throughout the year and then returned them.

The gun dance sequence followed. A procession of women entered the square and seated themselves in one of the houses, where they sang to the accompaniment of two men seated in front of them shaking gourd rattles. Two warriors with tomahawks danced halfway around a circle. The women then went to the mound in the center of the outer square, covered the mound, and resumed their chant. A stuffed figure was placed in each

[134] Payne, 1862, p. 23.

corner of the outer square enclosing the mound. Two parties of armed warriors crept up on the lateral sides of this "battle square," and the two warriors who had previously danced in the square ground crept up on the third side. These two men snatched two of the puppets, stabbed and scalped one, and carried off the second. The other two parties began a mock battle, in which a third puppet was shot and the fourth tomahawked, and finally both sides burst into the square. Disorder then subsided into a dance around the central mound on which the women were; they plunged into the square ground, ran around it lashing spectators with corn stalks, rushed back to the mound square, and then went to the river for the "going to water" ritual. Peace and a feast on the green corn ensued, and Payne noted considerable use of alcohol.

The third day, during most of which Payne was not present, "consisted, I was told, in the display of wives urging out their husbands to hunt deer."[135] When Payne returned toward evening, he saw the men returning with deer to present to the priests; the skins were returned with a prayer that these deer would be only a harbinger of abundance of game. Some dances were performed in the square ground that night.

On the fourth morning the medicine pots were no longer in the square ground. The first feature was a dance by all of the women dressed in their finest clothes; some of them wore terrapin-shell leg rattles under their long skirts. These women slowly danced around the central fire, and the last part of the line, consisting of women wearing the rattles, stopped facing the men and kept time for the rest. The first and last woman, each carrying a stick decorated with two pendant feathers, left the three circles of dancing women and danced in a fourth circuit outside of them. The old men made comments intended to surprise the women into laughter. At one point in each circuit the women turned to face the men. The women left the square at the end of the dance, but repeated the same performance in about an hour. The final phase of the ceremony, a rapid mixed

[135] *Ibid.*, p. 27.

dance, the dance of the olden time, concluded the festival, and Payne took his leave, having witnessed a ceremony that would next be performed on the alien soil of Indian Territory.

All of the previous references are to busks held before the removal of the Creeks to Oklahoma. The various towns continued to hold their green corn festivals, and a number of later accounts exist. In no case, however, has any observer made a complete study of the busk of any single town. The recent material has all been gathered and analyzed by Swanton[136] and shows little variation from the older data, except for some shortening and simplification of the rituals. The same variations in procedure that exist in the earlier accounts are noted. Rather than duplicate Swanton's material, I intend to limit this study to busks held east of the Mississippi and draw only on his information for some explanation of the concepts and symbolism underlying these ceremonies.

There are indications that certain features were always present in these ceremonies. Such traits include the square ground, the new fire ritual, the feather dance, the old dance, the gun dance, the preparation of the square ground, and the cleansing of the households, ritual disposal of earth removed from the square ground, the granting of amnesty to criminals, the use of herb medicines and purges, the priest's blowing into the medicine, fasting, the prohibition against salt, the taboo against eating green corn prior to the busk, the "going to water" ritual, all-night ritual observances, scarification (scratching) for punishment and as a ritual feature, animal dances, the seclusion of men in the square ground at certain times, direction and color symbolism, the appointment of "drivers" (as policemen), the erection of "sheds" on the sides of the square ground, a concluding feast on new corn and other foods, the use of gourd rattles, women's turtle-shell leg rattles, and water drum, the use of ibis or heron (?) wings, the setting of the date by male officials at a preliminary meeting, and a ceremonial hunt. These seem to be features which were always present in the busk. More than half

[136] Swanton, 1928*a*, pp. 534–621; 1928*b*, pp. 170–312.

of these elements are also noted in the Cherokee data, and several occur among the Delaware.

These features are also conspicuous in the recent accounts collected by Swanton. The tremendous amount of symbolism implicit in the busk has not been carefully or systematically studied by means of native informants, but has attracted some attention among later students, notably Speck and Swanton. From their data one may conclude that the square ground is a world symbol, often called "the big house" and "the rainbow." Such an interpretation would seem to equate the square ground with the ceremonial grounds of the Iroquois and Delaware areas; this idea and the direction-color symbolism of the square would sharply distinguish these rectangular structures from the round community structures used by Creek and Cherokee and noted by archaeologists in the Ohio Valley and other areas.

The busk is also referred to as a "peace time"; not necessarily in the sense of freedom from war but in the sense of peace within the community and between the community and supernatural powers. The dance content and specific features of the Creek and Cherokee green corn festivals suggest that one function of this ceremony is the placation and propitiation of the whole pantheon, including the sun, the fire, the thunders, the corn spirit, the spirits of plants, and the spirits of the animals upon which man preys. In the ceremonial inauguration of the new Creek year man renews his worn and strained spiritual relationships with his environment. Man's and woman's participation in Creek cultural life would also seem to be enacted in allegory. Thanksgiving, in the Iroquois sense, is not very conspicuous in available Creek data.

One notable feature is the injunction against eating the new corn prior to the festival, and the threat of disease as a punishment for the violation of this taboo. This not only determines the date for the ceremony, but may give a clue as to a primary and early significance of green corn ceremonialism; unfortunately, no information as to the existence of this taboo has survived in most areas.

The small amount of data available for the Tuskogee and Yuchi would indicate the essential Creek nature of their busks.[137] J. Francis Le Baron's Lake Pierce, Florida, note of 1881 contains some interesting references to the Seminole busk, which was doubtless very similar to the Creek ritual:

> They have a semi-religious annual festival in June or July, called the green corn dance, the new corn being then ripe enough to be eaten. Plurality of wives is forbidden by their laws. Tom Tiger, a fine-looking Indian, is said to have broken this rule by marrying two wives, for which misdemeaner he was banished from the tribe. He traveled about one hundred miles to the nearest tribe in the Everglades, and jumped unseen into the ring at the green corn dance. This procured him absolution, conformably to their laws.[138]

Although it has been claimed that the Choctaw were more agricultural than the Creek and other peoples of the Southeast,[139] there is remarkably little data on their ceremonialism. One of the authorities, Gideon Lincecum, who wrote a lengthy account of his Choctaw observations, mentioned a green corn dance,[140] but Alfred Wright, in 1828, denied that a green corn ritual was ever practised among the Choctaw.[141] Swanton's information from Choctaw informants indicates that the green corn ceremony, held in August, was primarily a time of law making and regulation, and lasted three days.[142] It seems probable that a festival somewhat like the Creek busk may have been observed among the Choctaw, but I have no data. The Chickasaw may also have held a green corn ceremony, but there is no information on this point, unless some of Adair's data about the busk pertain to Chickasaw.

THE NATCHEZ AND TRIBES OUTSIDE OF THE EASTERN WOODLANDS AREA

INFORMATION concerning the Natchez, although indicating a political and religious organization somewhat of the nature of a

---

[137] Speck, 1907; 1909b. [138] Gatschet, 1884, p. 73.
[139] Swanton, 1931, p. 46. [140] *Ibid.*, p. 21.
[141] *Ibid.*, p. 221. [142] *Ibid.*, pp. 225–26.

climax development, is drawn almost exclusively from the early French observers in Louisiana and consists mostly of accounts of the more spectacular aspects of Natchez life. Swanton has collected and discussed accounts of the green corn festival from five early sources.[143] His collection contains all of the data on this ceremony among the Natchez. It is not even certain whether some of this data actually pertains to the green corn festival. It is known from these accounts that a ceremony, generally observed in July, included a feast of first fruits and that certain traits were noted in its content. These include the use of a rectangular ceremonial ground, a new fire ceremony, four-direction symbolism, red and white symbolism, the use of special cabins on the sides of the square ground, all night dancing, the ball game, the use of a centerpost in the middle of the square, and the leaving of gifts at this post. The length of time noted for the ceremonies varies from one day to ten days.

After the destruction of the Natchez nation by the French in the early eighteenth century, some of the Natchez settled in the Creek and Cherokee country, and their descendents still exist among the Cherokee in Oklahoma. George Stiggins, a Creek of Natchez descent, wrote of these Natchez survivors in the latter part of the nineteenth century: "They keep the Busk festival in a very devout and sacred manner."[144] There seems to be no other data on the Natchez green corn festival, nor is there any indication of the influence the Natchez may have had on the busks of their neighbors, either before or after the Natchez settlements were located among other tribes. The little information which we do possess indicates strong resemblances between the Creek and Natchez green corn ceremonies.

The Quapaw and the Osage, Siouan tribes to the north of the Natchez, observed a green corn festival, according to Nuttall's information of 1819,[145] and Hunter suggested an Osage green corn festival,[146] but I can find no later information pertaining to these rituals. According to Joutel, the Caddoan Cenis of

---

[143] Swanton, 1911, pp. 110–23.   [144] Swanton, 1922, p. 315.
[145] Nuttall, 1821, pp. 96, 101.   [146] Will and Hyde, 1917, p. 260.

Texas also held some ritual at this time.[147] It might be expected that similar ceremonies occurred among the other agricultural tribes of the lower Mississippi Valley and Red River Valley, and among such more northerly agricultural tribes as the Hidatsa, Crow, Mandan, Arikara, Dakota, Penca, Pawnee, and Cheyenne, but no definite data on such ceremonies have been noted in the literature about these peoples. It seems impossible to say whether the hako rite of the Pawnee might have had any relationship to the ceremonies I have discussed.

Whitman's Oto report would indicate that a green corn ritual, held when the tribe returned from its early summer buffalo hunt, was a primary concern of the red bean medicine lodge. Members of this society ate the green corn and other crops only after holding a ritual, most details of which have not survived. Wilson noted, however, that all night dancing and the use of the red bean for a purge and purifying medicine preceded a feast on the new crop and the first buffalo meat of the season; these features have close parallels in the southeastern rites.[148] The buffalo-corn association and the general patterns of the society suggest the prairie corn complex, but the use of a corn medicine and the little information on the sequence suggest that a very modified version of the southeastern ritual existed here as a survival or as a restricted rite which had diffused from that direction. The red bean, widespread on the plains and prairie in other associations, may have been substituted here for the *Ilex* and other herb ingredients of the southeastern green corn ceremonies.

According to Schoolcraft, a Sioux group on the upper Mississippi held a green corn ceremony on August 2, 1820.[149] Later sources contain no clear information on such rituals in adjacent areas. In recent years the tremendous culture changes which were in process on the eastern plains and near-by regions in the period between the time of first European influence and the date of recent ethnographies have been noticed. Earlier students

[147] *Ibid.*, p. 259.   [148] Whitman, 1937, pp. 120–21.
[149] Schoolcraft, 1825, p. 319.

of the cultures of these areas could perhaps have still salvaged much data on the agricultural complexes of the plains and prairie regions, but with a few exceptions they emphasized the spectacular buffalo-hunting, military plains culture aspects of the unstable transitional cultures of these areas. The accounts of the Pawnee hako are good examples of an extinct rite inadequately recorded and interpreted, and, as with much of the Osage data, the descriptions are largely out of context and defy analysis.

Will and Hyde, in a most satisfactory study of the agriculture of the Upper Missouri area, concluded that "the elaborate ceremonies which marked the opening of the green corn season among many tribes appear to have been lacking among the Upper Missouri Indians."[150] Their data indicate that the green corn season was a time of feasting and plenty and that the extensive use of green corn in this area, both fresh and preserved for later use, is like that of the woodland peoples.[151] This preference throughout the eastern areas for foods prepared of unripe corn seems basic to the eastern maize complex and may be closely correlated with the general ritual emphasis in the East.

Jedidiah Morse, in 1820, wrote a lengthy account of the Miami, apparently from information supplied by Jean Baptiste Richardville, chief of the Miami nation.[152] Some of this is apparently a reliable record of Miami and Shawnee tradition, but more than half of it is plagiarized, with only the slightest alteration, from Hawkins' *Sketch of the Creek Country*, a work which was not published until eighteen years later (from a manuscript in the Alabama Historical Society). Possibly Morse was hoodwinked by some scholar in American ethnology; perhaps Morse used this manuscript material to swell out his account. Either theory seems unlikely, and this strange Miami description will no doubt remain a mystery. Of the sections copied from Hawkins, one describes the *"Green Corn Dance*, or,

[150] Will and Hyde, 1917, p. 116. [151] *Ibid.*, pp. 115-23, 147-58.
[152] Morse, 1822, pp. 96-106.

more properly speaking, 'the ceremony of thanksgiving for the first fruits of the earth'."[153] It is a description of a Creek busk by a person who had Hawkins' account at hand, but who had never seen the observance. Richardville was Peschewah ("the Lynx"), chief of the Miami nation, who died in 1841.[154] This account is perhaps copied from one of the several manuscript copies of Hawkins' paper which circulated among traders in the Creek area.

There is no information on similar rituals on the western Gulf coast. Gatschet and Swanton's Atakapa linguistic data might indicate such a festival among these people, but the reference is too vague to constitute even a suggestion.[155] In the Southwest the material available would indicate only slight resemblances between Pueblo agricultural ceremonialism and any eastern ritual complex.

The Mexican data would require more study than the Eastern Woodlands material to permit any comparisons. Ralph Beals has ventured some suggestions as to the possibilities of such comparative studies, and, although he seems more optimistic than his facts would warrant, his conjecture should be kept in mind:

> A number of ceremonial dances having similar purposes are found in northern Mexico. As suggested already, the ceremonies or dances may not themselves be the same or even of the same derivation, but the underlying idea may be from the same source. How close together they may actually be has been suggested by Fewkes's comparison of a Hopi and Aztec ceremony with the same object. (J. Walter Fewkes, "A Central American Ceremony Which Suggests the Snake Dance of Tusayan Villagers," *Amer. Anthropol.*, 6 [1893]: 285–305). Rain making and maize ceremonies are the most obvious and the most frequently referred to. They are, of course, rather obviously connected with agriculture and may have diffused along the track of the agricultural complex.[156]

In another place he listed his references to maize ceremonies as follows: Natchez, Tarahumare, Acaxee, Huichol, Tamauli-

---

[153] *Ibid.*, p. 105. [154] Hodge, 1911, 2: 234.
[155] Gatschet and Swanton, 1932, p. 23. [156] Beals, 1932, p. 133.

pas, Tarascans, Mexico, Maya, and Lacandone.[157] Again, the Mexican data do not indicate any relationships.

One may note that even in the Southeast, about which there seems to be an abundance of reliable information, an adequate understanding of aboriginal life can only be arrived at with much careful study of all available data. The place of the busk in the cultural life of the Southeast has not been carefully defined by earlier students. Recent conclusions of Swanton's illustrate the confusion that exists in the Southeast and sometimes contradicts the best source material on the area:

> Roughly the economic life of these Indians resolved themselves into a summer horticultural and fishing season and a winter hunting season. They had to return to their towns in time to plant the fields, after which some Indians continued to remain about the towns to keep watch over them, but the others dispersed in small parties to live upon fish, shell-fish, small game animals, berries, roots, and so on. The early corn also served to carry them over until July or August, when the new flour corn was ready to eat, the so-called green corn ceremony was held, and there was for a time abundance of food.[158]

Swanton said of roasted green corn:

> The late varieties of corn were eaten in this way only after the annual ceremony usually called the "green corn dance," the busk of the Creeks, had been celebrated.[159]

> Throughout the rest of the Southeast—except perhaps for a few bands living near the larger tribes, who are said to have specialized on hunting—corn, beans, pumpkins, and a few other vegetables were raised, and the fields where these grew usually determined the sites of the towns. This was because they required labor and protection and because most of the crop was stored for later consumption. Dried meat was also stored there, but it was never possible to tell where game animals were to be found, while the location of the field was definite. This, of course, meant that the people were generally in or near their villages in summer. They had to return to them in spring to plant, and a certain amount of cultivation was also necessary during the growing season, though the Indians did not worry themselves on this point

[157] *Ibid.*, p. 219.   [158] *Conference on Southeastern Pre-history*, 1935, p. 15.
[159] Swanton, 1946, p. 352.

as much as our farmers. However, it was also necessary to have someone watch the fields during the sprouting season to keep the ubiquitous crow and other birds in check. Between planting and harvest they did, however, often get time for a shorter hunt. After harvest they would remain in town until well toward winter to enjoy the produce of their fields and thus place it beyond the reach of human or animal depredation. This determined the period when the greatest feasts and ceremonies were held, the people being together and the maximum amount of food being available, the time of plenty was usually inaugurated by a special ceremony known to English-speaking people popularly as "the green corn dance," though it might be more accurately defined as a feast of first fruits, the ceremony being intended to insure continued supplies of plant and animal food during the ensuing year and along with them the health and prosperity of the partakers.

As the harvest was seldom sufficient to last—nor was it expected to last—until another crop came in, the Indians were obliged to seek natural food supplies elsewhere and, since such supplies were not usually concentrated, this meant that the people themselves scattered about in camps where they remained until planting time. Along the coast food supplies were usually more plentiful, though the same scattering took place in search of favorite fishing grounds. Here the annual spring runs of herring and other fish brought about concentrations of population at fishing stations on the rivers, particularly those at the edge of the Piedmont Plateau. But as these took place near the planting season, the interruption of the winter hunt occasioned by them was relatively small. Among littoral people, however, fishing tended to take the place of the summer hunt. Nevertheless, even the inland tribes were not without opportunities to enjoy a fish diet in summer, for they had fish traps led to by converging lines of rocks, and it was then they resorted to the poisoning of fish in pools in the shrunken streams, or dragged them for the same purpose.[160]

One short description written by Benjamin Hawkins is of considerable interest because it suggests far better the role of agriculture and the maize complex in the sedentary town life of the Creeks.

I chose the river path that I might have a view of the Indian fields, their mode of culture and the quality of the lands. The first

---

[160] Swanton, 1946, pp. 256–57.

4 miles were high and open sound low grounds, subject to inundations only in the seasons of floods which happen once in 15 or 16 years, the river is also subject to annual overflowings, but always in the winter season, generally in March; the next 8 miles is mostly canebrake land, very rich, much of it under cultivation, the corn planted in hills, not regular, about 5 feet from each other, and from 5 to 10 stalks in a hill, near every small division of corn they have a patch of beans stuck with cane. The margins on the river under cultivation is from one hundred to 200 yards wide, then the land becomes a rich swamp for 400 to 600 yards, this when reclaimed must be valuable for rice or corn, the river never subject to freshes in the spring or summer. I saw one conic mound in this low land 30 feet diameter, ten feet high, it stands near the river. The towns standing on the right bank of the river, there are at several places large peach trees, and a few summer huts to shelter the labourers in summer against rain, and the guards who watch the crops whilst it grows to protect it against every thing that may be injurious to it. Many of them move over their families, reside in the fields whilst the crop is growing and when it is made they gather the whole and move into town.

During this season, they show in a particular manner their hospitality, they call to all travelers, particularly white travelers and give them fruit, melons and food. If there is a necessity the women and children eat of the young corn before the busk, but the men do not.[161]

CORN ORIGIN MYTHS

In the Southwest corn is either considered as always having been in existence or accounted for in the emergence stories, and a number of female spirits, the corn maidens, are known in the folklore and literature. In the Eastern Woodlands a mythical, premaize period is recognized, and one myth of the origin of corn is told with considerable uniformity throughout the area.

According to some traditions the corn was carried from the South in the ear of a crow. This story is recorded for the New York City area and for the Narranganset and Iroquois,[162] but is not recorded for the rest of the area. In Tuggle's version of the

[161] Hawkins, 1917, pp. 41–42.
[162] Williams, 1827, p. 85; Wolley, 1902, p. 42; Converse, 1908, p. 63.

Creek story of the Corn Mother,[163] the birds carried off and ate the corn which the Corn Mother's son had hidden in a corn crib, but the crows dropped some, which people found and planted.

Throughout most of the Eastern Woodlands, however, the Corn Mother was the mythical being who was transformed into the maize. Swanton, in a recent discussion of the ethnological problems of the Southeast, has suggested the significance of this folktale:

There are traces also of a worship of the Corn Mother and certain other spirits of a general character associated particularly with the Busk. This busk was always held when the flour corn of the new crop was first fit for use, and practically every tribe in the Southeast had some special ceremony connected with this event, while the Creeks and Natchez, at least, seem to have had an extended series of ceremonies lasting all summer.[164]

Swanton has collected several versions of this tale from Creek informants and several from persons of Natchez descent who still had some knowledge of the Natchez language.[165] Although most of these represent clipped versions of what must have been a more complete story, there is little difference between the Creek and Natchez variants, and both are probably derived from the same tradition. Whether this indicates the near identity of the Creek and Natchez Corn Mother tales, or whether all of these stories are of Creek origin, is a difficult question, but the latter explanation seems more probable.

These stories contain a central narrative in which the son of the Corn Mother tends to be disobedient. She obtained corn and beans from a corn crib whenever it was needed, and he became curious about her source of supply. He watched her through a crack in the wall of the crib and saw her shaking the corn from her body into a basket. He thought the food was merely excrement and refused to eat it. She realized what had happened and sent him out hunting for food. He looked beyond

[163] Swanton, 1929, pp. 16-17.
[164] *Conference on Southeastern Pre-history*, 1935, p. 19.
[165] Swanton, 1929, pp. 9-17, 230-34.

the mountains and felt an urge to travel into the marvelous land beyond. His mother made him a flute and a headdress of snakes and bluejays (and sometimes parakeets). She told him that he must kill her and burn her body in their house. After disposing of her, he set out into the world, where he engaged in a series of adventures in which he overcame the trickster rabbit and women with toothed vaginas, and found a wife. He demonstrated certain magical powers (and showed some traits of the culture hero) and returned with his wife to harvest the corn. The same story occurs without the corn-origin motif.[166] In some versions the Corn Mother's son was the orphan born from a blood clot or "thrown away" blood,[167] and in one version the Corn Mother's body is dragged on the ground, from which corn springs up.[168] In none of these versions do the twin culture heroes play the role of the orphan in this tale. The twins play major roles in other tales; the orphan of the Corn Mother tale definitely suggests the afterbirth boy or the blood-clot boy of the twins, but is not identified with him in the available material.

An interesting dichotomy is indicated in the Creek area. Farther north in the Eastern Woodlands the twin culture heroes are instrumental in the origin of corn; on the plains and in other areas twin culture heroes function in similar ways, but the Corn Mother story is absent. In the Creek area, and also among the Seminole, the two features exist side by side, but are not incorporated into one tale.[169]

Several versions of the Cherokee tale have been published, and although there is some disagreement in detail between different versions, a generalized résumé of the story is possible.[170] A man and his wife (kanati', "the hunter," and se·lu', "corn") monopolized all of the game and vegetable crops in the world. A son was born to them, and his wild twin was transformed from

[166] Ibid., pp. 17–19, 234–39.   [167] Ibid., pp. 10, 13–14, 16–17.
[168] Ibid., p. 14.
[169] Ibid., pp. 2–7, 133–34, 222–30; Greenlee, 1945, p. 141; Reichard, 1921.
[170] Mooney, 1888, p. 98; 1900, p. 242–45, 248, 431–34; Witthoft, 1946b, pp. 217–18.

the thrown-away placenta or from blood. The wild boy was finally captured and the two boys were raised together; the "tame" boy being well-behaved, the "wild" boy demonstrating the well-known perversities of the trickster culture hero and taking the lead in their escapades.

The twins, apparently by accident, released all of the game which their father had impounded in a cave, thus making it available for man. They spied on their mother in the corn house and saw her shaking the corn from her body. The boys, believing that she was tricking them into eating excrement, killed her. When her body was dragged about in the clearing, corn sprang up. Originally, the corn grew and matured overnight, provided that the people stayed awake all night and danced, but this requirement was once overlooked, and ever since corn has taken much longer to grow. The two boys set off in search of their father, who fled to the West when he learned of the death of his wife. In their journey they overcame a number of menaces to humanity, and, finally arriving at their father's abode, assumed their duties as the Thunders.

I have found no record of this story among the Delaware and their neighbors, but the Corn Mother story is a major Iroquois explanation of the origin of corn. Whereas the Cherokee tale exists as an isolated myth, the Iroquois version has been incorporated into a cosmogenic myth cycle, all the parts of which do not occur together in any single published version (thus probably indicating some flexibility in the content and sequence). The Iroquoian Corn Mother story has also been recorded separately in other contexts.[171]

According to the usual Iroquois version, maize grew from the body of the woman who gave birth to the Creator and his evil-minded twin.[172] This Corn Mother, in turn, was the daughter of a pregnant woman who was let down from heaven, and for whom the earth was formed by the animals (the earth-diver story). The Corn Mother was impregnated by a man from the

[171] Hewitt, 1918, pp. 642–63.
[172] Parker, 1910, pp. 36–37; Cornplanter, 1938, pp. 26–30.

heavens, who, according to my Cayuga informants, laid a sharp arrow and a blunt arrow on her body, these forming the good and bad brothers. When the twins were ready to be born, the evil-minded one went in the direction of a beam of light, so killing his mother, but the Creator was born naturally. The maize sprang from her body. Flint, the evil-minded brother, and the Creator grew up together, always engaged in struggle. The Creator made man and many useful animals and plants; Flint made carniverous animals and enemies to man. Finally, the Creator overcame his brother (in the bowl game, according to some variants), and thus ensured the continuance of man and his world.

One may note here that the Creator and his brother actually are the twin culture heroes and are equivalents of the Cherokee Thunders. The specific modifications of the theme of this tale in various areas present a most interesting subject of study. Similar twin culture heroes played a comparable role in the mythology of southern New England,[173] but I have no data on equivalent corn origin stories from this area.

In northern New England beyond the area of green corn ceremonialism appears the last dim outline of the Corn Mother myth. This story, recorded for both Malecite and Penobscot, may be a recent accession from the Iroquois; at any rate, it seems to mark the limit of the diffusion of the Corn Mother belief. According to Speck's and Mechling's data,[174] a woman who magically produced corn from her body grew old and was about to die. She told her husband that he should clear land around their cabin and then drag her body over the cleared ground. He did this after she died and was dismayed to find her body torn off in shreds by the stumps. The maize grew in the area where the body had been dragged.

Will and Hyde have collected together the data on corn origin stories from the tribes of the Upper Missouri and adjacent re-

[173] Information personally supplied by Eva Butler, who is engaged in a study of the mythology of southern New England.
[174] Speck, 1940, pp. 194–95; Mechling, 1914, pp. 87–88.

gions and have pointed out characteristic features of the corn origin stories of these areas.[175] The corn people origin tales in this region suggest the southwestern corn traditions; the female corn spirits and the Corn Mother suggest the Eastern Woodlands belief, although the twin tales do not occur in this association. The Corn Mother contrasts sharply with the male corn spirit of the central Algonkian area, who is an actor in tales suggestive of prairie traditions. Central Algonkian social patterns are reflected in the corn traditions and usage as are those of the prairie and Eastern Woodlands cultures. It is curious to note that the central Algonkian corn origin legends have diffused to the Iroquois and are found as isolated tales in the collections.

CONCLUSION

ONE of the recurrent features of the maize complex of the Eastern Woodlands is the correlation of a major ritual with the ripening of corn. Such green corn ceremonies were generally more important than planting or harvest rituals and in the Southeast and among the Iroquois are known to have marked major divisions of the annual cycle. Such rituals appear to be specific to the Eastern Woodlands, roughly to coincide with the distribution of other traits characteristic of the Eastern Woodlands maize complex, and to differ significantly from any aspects of southwestern or Mexican ceremonialism. Available data indicate the distribution of this trait from the southern New England tribes to Seminole, and west to Natchez, Quapaw, Osage, and eastern Dakota. It is not recorded for many groups within this area, however, and, in view of the sparse data for many tribes, the boundaries cannot be accurately determined. Emphasis on this specific rite seems to be correlated with the extensive utilization of green corn within this area.

Green corn ceremonies have survived to the present, often in attenuated form, among Iroquois, Cherokee, Creek, and Seminole. The Cherokee ritual seems to have been subject to the

[175] Will and Hyde, 1917, pp. 210–36.

most extensive modification in recent years, but there are indications that considerable change may have occurred in the ceremonies of other groups in the past century or two of European contact. Observations on such trends in Creek busks have been previously noted. The general poverty of information for other ethnic groups is the major obstacle to a trait distribution study of green corn rituals.

Within the Eastern Woodlands, the largest part of the area is linked by such traits as the correlation of the ritual with the stage of maize ripening at a preliminary meeting, the rectangular ceremonial area as a stratified world symbol, new fire ceremonialism, the burning of tobacco, the use of tally sticks or tally notches to set the date in advance, a four-day ritual, all night dancing, calendric significance of the ritual, the distinction between ritual and social dances, the Corn Mother myth as the origin story for the ceremony, and separate men's and women's parts as well as mixed functions.

In the Southeast the green corn festival is most conspicuous and most elaborate. Variation between the rituals of Yuchi, Tuskigee, Alabama, and Creek is no greater than variation between those of various Creek towns. The Cherokee ritual is very closely related, and data from the Cherokee-Southeastern area indicate the closest correspondences in detail for any sizeable area of the Eastern Woodlands. Some of the traits shared between the Creek busk and the Cherokee ceremony are the open square ground surrounded by sheds, use of an emetic followed by herb medicines, belief in the production of intestinal worms from corn and the use of herb medicines as prophylaxis during the ritual, injunction against the eating of corn prior to the ceremony, taboo against salt during the ritual, green corn festival as the new year rite, vegetable and animal burnt offerings, a ritual hunt, fasting, direction—color symbolism, gourd rattles, women's turtle-shell leg rattles, animal dances, a gun dance, some dances held outside of the square ground, the square ground consecrated, swept, or covered with fresh earth and restricted, the "going to water" ritual, the ceremony as a time and place of amnesty, use of ritual jargon and archaic forms, appointment of "drivers" or policemen, green tree branches carried in ritual.

In the Southeast animal dances are conspicuous features in green corn rituals. These dances are apparently concerned with the propitiation of the spirits of hunted animals and are comparable to the hunting and medicinal songs and formulas which also serve this function.[176] Other first fruits rites were held, for example, a bean ritual. Animal dances are also a part of the Delaware ritual, but are unimportant in the Iroquois ceremony. Animal foods were apparently sacrificed in the Delaware ceremony, as in the Southeast, but not in the Iroquois (and southern New England?) rites. The Delaware and New England and coastal Algonkians held first fruits rites which were not concerned with agriculture; venison, fish, and other animal foods were involved in separate ceremonies initiating their seasonal usage. The green corn festival seems to be the sole Iroquois first fruits rite and is only incidentally concerned with nonagricultural economic activities. The southern Algonkian first fruits observances are curiously reminiscent of northern Algonkian animal ceremonialism;[177] they also suggest specific animistic attitudes toward the animal world which are characteristic of Creek and Cherokee but not strongly developed in Iroquois.

Like many other traits of the Eastern Woodlands maize complex, green corn ceremonialism apparently was not derived from the Southwest or from Mexico. In terms of importance and complexity, its place of origin and strongest development would appear to be in the Southeast. Rituals involving the first seasonal usage of each major animal food are present in both non-agricultural and agricultural areas of the Eastern Woodlands and may provide the substratum for agricultural rites. The Indians of the Southeast still preserve elements of such animal rituals within green corn festivals, and the southern Algonkians

---

[176] Speck, 1907, pp. 135–36, gives the best discussion of this important aspect.

[177] Flannery, 1939, pp. 135–36, 184, 192; 1946, p. 267.

held both corn and animal first fruits rites. The Iroquois, further from the presumable center of the maize complex, held only a green corn festival not directly concerned with hunting. Possibly, green corn ritualism may in part represent a transference and remodification of earlier hunting ceremonialism in the Southeast, rather than a part of an agricultural complex which diffused to the Eastern Woodlands.

LITERATURE CITED

ADAIR, JAMES
>1930 History of the American Indians. Johnson City, Tenn.: Watauga Press.

BARTRAM, WILLIAM
>1791 Travels Through North and South Carolina. Philadelphia: James and Johnson.
>1853 Observations on the Creek and Cherokee Indians. (Ed. by E. G. Squier.) Trans. Amer. Ethnol. Soc., 3, Pt. 1: 1-81.

BEALS, RALPH
>1932 Comparative Ethnology of Northern Mexico before 1750. Ibero-Americana, 2, Berkeley, Calif: Univ. Calif. Press.

BEVERLEY, ROBERT
>1705 The History and Present State of Virginia. London: R. Parker. 4 vols.

BRICKELL, JOHN
>1844 Narrative of John Brickell's Captivity Among the Delaware Indians. *In:* American Pioneer. Cincinnati: Logan Hist. Soc., 1842. 1: 43-56.

CARTER, GEORGE F.
>1945 Plant Geography and Culture History in the American Southwest. Viking Fund Publ. Anthropol., 5.

CHAMBERLAIN, M.
>1904 Indians. Acadiensis, 4: 280-95.

Conference on Southeastern Pre-history. Birmingham, Alabama, Dec. 18-20,
>1932   1935. Washington: National Research Council.

CONVERSE, HARRIET
>1908 Myths and Legends of the New York State Iroquois. (Ed. by A. C. Parker.) New York State Mus. Bull., 125.

CORNPLANTER, JESSE J.
>1938 Legends of the Longhouse. Philadelphia: J. B. Lippincott Co.

DENTON, DANIEL
>1937 A Brief Description of New York. New York: Facsimile Text Soc.

Explorations and Field Work of the Smithsonian Institution for 1913.
   1913   Smithsonian Misc. Coll., 63, Pt. 8. *Ibid.*, 1914, 65, Pt. 6.
FENTON, WILLIAM N.
   1936 An Outline of Seneca Ceremonies at Coldspring Longhouse. Yale Univ. Publ. Anthropol., 9.
   1941 Tonawanda Longhouse Ceremonies Ninety Years after Lewis Henry Morgan. Bull. Bur. Amer. Ethnol., 128: 140–66.
   MS *a* Green Corn Festival at Coldspring Longhouse. MS in possession of Dr. Fenton.
   MS *b* Green Corn Festival at Newtown Longhouse. MS in possession of Dr. Fenton.
   MS *c* Outline of Onondaga Ceremonies, Six Nations Reserve, Ontario, Canada. MS in possession of Dr. Fenton.
FLANNERY, REGINA
   1939 An Analysis of Coastal Algonquian Culture. Catholic Univ. of Amer. Anthropol. Ser., 7.
   1946 The Culture of the Northeastern Indian Hunters: A Descriptive Survey. *In* Frederick Johnson, Ed., Man in Northeastern North America. Papers Robt. S. Peabody Found. Archeol., 3: 263–71.
FOSTER, GEORGE E.
   1885 Se-quo-yah, the American Cadmus and Modern Moses. Philadelphia: Indian Rights Association.
FROBENIUS, LEO
   1909 The Childhood of Man. (Trans. by A. H. Keane.) Philadelphia: J. B. Lippincott Co.
GATSCHET, ALBERT S.
   1884 A Migration Legend of the Creeks. Brinton's Lib. Aboriginal Amer. Lit. Philadelphia: D. G. Brinton. No. 4.
GATSCHET, ALBERT S., and JOHN R. SWANTON.
   1932 A Dictionary of the Atakapa Language. Bull. Bur. Amer. Ethnol., 108.
GILBERT, WILLIAM H.
   1943 The Eastern Cherokee. Bull. Bur. Amer. Ethnol., 133: 169–413.
GREENLEE, ROBERT F.
   1945 Folktales of the Florida Seminole. Journ. Amer. Folklore, 58: 138–44.
GROVER, THOMAS
   1904 An Account of Virginia. (Reprinted from the Phila. Trans. Royal Soc., June 20, 1678.) Oxford.
GYLES, JOHN
   1850 Captivity. *In:* Samuel G. Drake, Indian Captivities or Life in the Wigwam. Auburn, N. Y.: Derby and Miller. Pp. 75–109.
HARRINGTON, M. R.
   1921 Religion and Ceremonies of the Lenape. Mus. Amer. Indian, Heye Found., Indian Notes and Monogr., Misc., No. 19.

1938 Dickon among the Lenape Indians. Philadelphia: John G. Winston Co.

HARIOT, THOMAS
1895 Narrative of the First English Plantation in America. (Reprint) London: Bernard Quaritch.

HAWKINS, BENJAMIN
1848 A Sketch of the Creek Country in 1799. Col. Georgia Hist. Soc., Pt. 1: 3.
1917 Letters of Benjamin Hawkins, 1796–1806. *Ibid.*, 9.

HECKEWELDER, JOHN
1876 History, Manners, and Customs of the Indian Nations. (Ed. by W. C. Reichel.) Mem. Hist. Soc. Pa., 12.

HEWITT, J. N. B.
1918 Seneca Fiction, Legends, and Myths. Ann. Rept. Bur. Amer. Ethnol., 32.

HICKS, CHARLES
1818 Manners, Customs, etc. of the Cherokee Indians. Published in the Raleigh Register and clipping preserved in Bur. Amer. Ethnol. Scrapbk., 1: 354.

HODGE, FREDERICK W.
1911 Handbook of American Indians North of Mexico. Bur. Amer. Ethnol. Bull., 30.

HODGSON, ADAM
1923 Remarks During a Journey Through North America. New York: J. Seymour.

Indian Papers I. MS in Connecticut State Library, Hartford, Conn.

JAMESON, ANNA M.
1839 Winter Studies and Summer Rambles in Canada. New York: Wiley and Putnam. 3 vols.

LALEMANT, JEROME
1898a Relation of 1640. *In:* R. G. Thwaites, The Jesuit Relations and Allied Documents. Cleveland: Burrows Bros. 19: 77–267.
1898b Letter of 1645. *Ibid.*, 28: 39–101.

LAWSON, JOHN
1714 The History of Carolina. London: W. Taylor and J. Baker.

LINTON, RALPH
1924 The Significance of Certain Traits in North American Maize Culture. Amer. Anthropol., n.s., 26: 345–49.

LOSKIEL, GEORGE H.
1794 History of the Mission of the United Brethren among the Indians in North America. (Trans. by C. I. LaTrobe.) London: Brethren's Society for the Furtherance of the Gospel.

LOUGHRIDGE, R. M., and DAVID M. HODGE.
1890 English and Muskokee Dictionary. St. Louis: J. T. Smith.

MECHLING. W. H.
 1914 Malecite Tales. Mem. Canad. Dept. Mines, 49.
MILFORT, LE CLERK
 1802 Memoir du coup d'oeil rapide sur mes differens voyages et mon sejour dans la Nation Creck. Paris: Giguet et Michaud.
MOONEY, JAMES
 1888 Myths of the Cherokees. Journ. Amer. Folklore, 1: 97–108.
 1900 Myths of the Cherokee. Ann. Rept. Bur. Amer. Ethnol., 19: 5–548.
 MS*a* MS 2235, Bur. Amer. Ethnol. Arch.
 MS*b* MS 3848, *ibid.*
MOONEY, JAMES, and FRANZ OLBRECHTS.
 1932 The Swimmer Manuscript. Bull. Bur. Amer. Ethnol., 99.
MORGAN, LEWIS H.
 1851 League of the Ho-dé-no-sau-nee, or Iroquois. Rochester: Sage and Brother.
MORSE, JEDIDIAH
 1822 Report to the Secretary of War of the United States, on Indian Affairs. New Haven, Conn.: Howe and Spaulding.
NUTTALL, THOMAS
 1821 A Journal of Travels into the Arkansa Territory During the Year 1819. Philadelphia: T. H. Palmer.
PARKER, ARTHUR
 1910 Iroquois Use of Maize and Other Food Plants. New York State Mus. Bull., 144.
 1913 The Code of Handsome Lake, the Seneca Prophet. *Ibid.*, 163.
PAYNE, JOHN HOWARD
 1862 The Green Corn Dance. Continental Mo., 1: 17–29.
 MS*a* Manuscript including copy of Bartram's Observations, untitled. Pennsylvania Historical Society Library, Philadelphia.
 MS*b* Manuscript relating to southeastern Indians, 14 vols., Ayer Collection, Newberry Library, Chicago.
PENN, WILLIAM
 1852 A Letter from William Penn, Proprietary and Govenour of Pennsylvania in America to the Committee of the Free Society of Traders of that Province, Residing in London. Reprinted in Samuel M. Janney, The Life of William Penn. Philadelphia: Lippincott, Grambo, and Co. Pp. 227–38.
REICHARD, GLADYS
 1921 Literary Types and Dissemination of Myths. Journ. Amer. Folklore, 36: 269–307.
 1829 Rhode Island Historical Collections, 2. Providence, R. I.
RITCHIE, WILLIAM A.
 1944 The Pre-Iroquoian Occupations of New York. Rochester Mus. Mem., 1.

Ruttenber, E. M.
    1872 History of the Indian Tribes of Hudson's River. ... Albany, N. Y.: J. Munsell.
Schoolcraft, Henry R.
    1825 Travels in the Central Portions of the Mississippi Valley. New York: Collins and Hannay.
    1860 Historical and Statistical Information, Respecting the History, Condition, and Prospects of the Indian Tribes of the United States. Philadelphia: J. B. Lippincott and Co. 6 vols.
Skinner, Alanson
    1915a Indians of Manhattan Island. Amer. Mus. Nat. Hist. Guide Leaflet, 41.
    1915b Indians of Greater New York. Little Histories of North American Indians, Cedar Rapids, Ia.
Smith, John
    1907 Generall Historie of Virginia, New England, and the Summer Islands. Glasgow: J. MacLehose and Sons, 2 vols.
Speck, F. G.
    1907 Creek Indians of Taskigi Town. Mem. Amer. Anthropol. Assn., 2: 99–164.
    1909a Notes on the Mohegan and Niantic Indians. Anthropol. Papers Amer. Mus. Nat. Hist., 3: 181–210.
    1909b Ethnology of the Yuchi Indians. Univ. Penna. Anthropol. Publ. Univ. Mus., 1.
    1924 Ethnic Position of the Southeastern Algonkian. Amer. Anthropol., n.s., 26: 184–200.
    1928 Native Tribes and Dialects of Connecticut. Ann. Rept. Bur. Amer. Ethnol., 43: 199–287.
    1937 Oklahoma Delaware Ceremonies, Feasts and Dances. Mem. Amer. Phil. Soc., No. 7.
    1940 Penobscot Man. Philadelphia: Univ. Penna.
    1942 The Tutelo Spirit Adoption Ceremony. Harrisburg, Pa.: Penna. Hist. Comm.
    1945 The Celestial Bear Comes Down to Earth. Reading Public Mus. Sci. Publ., 7.
    MSa Eastern Cherokee Songs and Dances. MS in possession of Doctor Speck.
    MSb Cayuga Ceremonies. In press, Univ. of Penna. Press.
Squier, E. G.
    1851 Antiquities of the State of New York. Buffalo: Geo. H. Derby and Co.
Stiles, Ezra
    1916 Extracts from the Itineraries and Other Miscellanies. (Ed. by F. B. Dexter.) New Haven: Yale Univ. Press.

SWANTON, J. R.
    1911 Indian Tribes of the Lower Mississippi Valley and the Adjacent Coast of the Gulf of Mexico. Bull. Bur. Amer. Ethnol., 43.
    1922 Early History of the Creek Indians and Their Neighbors. *Ibid.*, 73.
    1928*a* Creek Social Organization and Usages. Ann. Rept. Bur. Amer. Ethnol., 42: 23–472.
    1928*b* Religious Beliefs and Medical Practices of the Creek Indians. *Ibid.*, pp. 473–672.
    1929 Myths and Tales of the Southeastern Indians. Bull. Bur. Amer. Ethnol., 88.
    1931 Source Material for the Social and Ceremonial Life of the Choctaw Indians. *Ibid.*, 103.
    1932 The Green Corn Dance. Chron. of Okla., 10: 170–95.
    1946 The Indians of the Southeastern United States. Bull. Bur. Amer. Ethnol., 137.

THOMAS, GABRIEL
    1900 An Historical and Geographical Account of the Province and Country of Pennsylvania. Reprinted in Liberty Bell Leaflets, 5, 6. Philadelphia: Sower.

TUTTLE, SARAH
    1833 Letters and Conversations on the Cherokee Mission. 2d ed.; Boston: Amer. Sabbath School Union.

WASSENAER, NICOLAES VAN
    1850 Description and First Settlement of New Neatherland. *In* E. B. O'Callaghan, Documentary History of New York. Albany, N. Y. 3: 27–48 (trans. Wassenaer, Historie van Europa. Amsterdam, 1621–32).

WAUBUNO, CHIEF (John B. Wampum)
    n.d. The Traditions of the Delaware, as Told by Chief Waubuno. London.

WEBB, WILLIAM S., and C. S. SNOW
    1945 The Adena People. Univ. Ky. Publ. Anthropol., 6.

WHITE, JOHN
    Photographs of the original drawings (British Museum) issued by the Bur. Amer. Ethnol.

WHITMAN, WILLIAM
    1937 The Oto. Columbia Univ. Contrib. Anthropol., 27.

WILL, GEORGE F., and GEORGE E. HYDE.
    1917 Corn among the Indians of the Upper Missouri. Little Histories of North American Indians. St. Louis. No. 5.

WILLIAMS, ROGER
    1827 A Key into the Language of America. Rhode Island Hist. Coll., 1: 17–165.

WISSLER, CLARK
    1922 The American Indian. New York: Oxford Univ. Press.

WITTHOFT, JOHN
    1946a Cayuga Midwinter Festival. New York Folklore Quart., 2: 24–39.
    1946b The Cherokee Green Corn Festival and the Green Corn Medicine. Journ. Wash. Acad. Sci., 36: 213–19.

WOLLEY, CHARLES
    1902 Two Years' Journal in New York. Cleveland: Burrows Bros.

ZEIZBERGER, DAVID
    1910 History of the Northern American Indians. (Ed. by A. B. Hulbert, and W. N. Schwarze.) Columbus, Ohio: Ohio State Archaeol. and Hist. Soc.